TEACHING RACISM
OR TACKLING IT?

MULTICULTURAL STORIES FROM WHITE
BEGINNING TEACHERS

1858561280

TEACHING RACISM –
OR TACKLING IT?
MULTICULTURAL STORIES FROM WHITE
BEGINNING TEACHERS

Russell Jones

Trentham Books

First published in 1999 by Trentham Books Limited

Trentham Books Limited
Westview House
734 London Road
Oakhill
Stoke on Trent
Staffordshire
England ST4 5NP

British Cataloguing in Publication Data
A catalogue record for this book is available from the British Library
ISBN: 1 85856 129 9 (pb)
ISBN: 1 85856 128 0 (hb)

Designed and typeset by Trentham Print Design Ltd., Chester
and printed in Great Britain by The Cromwell Press Ltd., Wiltshire

Contents

I would like to thank several people formally for their part in the production of this book. John Robinson and Ian Stronach were a constant source of challenge, inspiration and support during the period of research. As a supervisory team I do not think I could have asked for a more stimulating combination. Phil Hodkinson's advice from the sidelines always seemed timely and insightful. Gillian Klein's advice in the production of the book was sensitive, supportive and insightful. I am, of course, indebted to the students, Headteachers, teachers, mentors and university lecturers who contributed to the interviews.

Val was, as ever, entirely responsible for making the whole enterprise possible.

This book is for Sophie.

Introduction

This book explores how students in predominantly or exclusively white areas of the country come to understand issues of ethnicity during the course of their training to be primary teachers. Chris Gaine titled his book *No Problem Here*, to indicate the persistent concept that schools with no ethnic minority pupils have no 'problem' to address and the persistent problematising of race. Today one in twenty people living in Britain is of African, Caribbean or Asian descent, more than half of them born here. In some city schools, ethnic minority pupils make up a significant, sometimes even major, part of the roll. The research which underpins this book unpicks the concept of 'no problem here' and reveals what this means for beginning teachers who find themselves in schools which deny that race issues exist. All are white students trained in an exclusively white university context and working in predominantly white classrooms. Working alongside white teachers who deny that race and ethnicity are relevant to children's experience of schooling and receiving training which marginalises issues of equality and ethnicity, these young people have few resources or strategies with which to tackle overt and institutional racism in their classrooms.

The teachers being prepared to teach in the new millennium receive very different training to that experienced by most teachers now working in schools. Legislation over recent years has sought control over what is taught to intending teachers and over the nature of their training experiences. Issues of assessment, recording, reporting, classroom management and so on are paramount. In the drive to meet these new criteria, certain aspects of teacher training have been downgraded or lost, leaving considerable gaps in students' understandings about children and their schools. Legislation has now put universities into partnerships with schools, and shifted the balance of training towards the classroom and learning 'on the job'. It seems to be presumed that longer periods spent in schools equates with higher standards of teaching and that the student learns the whole business of teaching through struc-tured school experience and professional osmosis. Racial equality in education is strongly affected by this shift in initial teacher train-ing (ITE), so this book contextualises current practices in multi-cultural education within the business of teacher training. How issues of ethnicity are perceived in exclusively white classrooms is explored by means of scrutinising how teachers are currently trained to work in those classrooms.

Somewhere along this journey, the delicate balance between university-based education and school-based experience has altered so that less knowledge is conveyed about the social context of childhood, and more about the beauraucratic and technical pro-cesses of meeting the needs of the National Curriculum. While the book focuses on the specific issue of racial justice, there are further, tightly interrelated issues of class, gender and disability which feature in the 'stories' that follow. These stories relate how students are qualifying as primary teachers with little or no under-standing about the lives of children, the social forces which affect children's learning or the strategies needed to ensure that the best possible teaching and learning experiences are afforded to all children in all schools.

The 'stories' from two cohorts of beginning teachers describe their experiences as they desperately try to make sense of the teaching and learning situations in which they find themselves, situations which are clearly of desperate importance to the children involved, but for which the beginning teachers (and in some cases their mentors and established teachers) have no training, no knowledge and no strategies for solution.

The research on which this book draws frequently alludes to the 'white highlands'. This term has a colonial history, but it has also been used (unproblematically) to describe the kinds of 'white' schools discussed by Chris Gaine. Gaine examined mainly white secondary schools, looking at how multicultural education was easily dismissed as irrelevant because of low numbers of ethnic minority children on roll. I use the term 'white highlands' to refer to the majority of the schools discussed here, which contained no representatives of minority cultures whatsoever. Some readers may find this difficult to believe, but it was indeed so. Virtually all the schools where my sample students worked were exclusively white, although a few had one or two ethnic minority children, and one school attracted an ethnic minority population of between five and ten per cent (and is discussed in 'Helen's Story'). The 'white highlands' of Britain's schools meant just that; a group of schools, usually (but not necessarily) in rural areas, where the children and staff are all white.

While I personally grew up in an ethnically diverse social and educational context, my entire teaching career was spent in schools in the 'white highlands'. In the eight years of my primary teaching career I came across three black children and never saw a black teacher. The students I set out to study were also white, as were all their lecturers at their universities and all the teachers they worked alongside in schools. This was not part of the research design. In the six years I worked as a part-time lecturer at the two institutions under scrutiny I taught one student who was Dutch and another who had an English mother and a Bangladeshi father. I never met an ethnic minority lecturer, teacher or mentor. In the vast majority of cases out in schools, these students never had the opportunity to work alongside a black or Asian child, and certainly had no contact with an ethnic minority teacher. Occasionally they would be sent to schools where there were a very small number of children from ethnic minority communities. By bringing together this research data in the form of stories, it becomes possible to look beyond the surface of mere lack of equal opportunities provision in ITE and to reveal what this actually means for the beginning teachers who face significant (and sometimes violent) issues in their classrooms – and for the children in their charge.

Chapter I

Twenty years of multicultural decline

Multicultural education has had a difficult task justifying its existence in recent years. The absence of any educational input on issues of race means that many teachers and learners cannot recognise the importance of acknowledging and understanding ethnic status in the classroom, nor do they have professional strategies to combat racism in the education system. For us to understand the beginning teachers in this book, we need to know the context, and this is shaped by multicultural and anti-racist education and the current educational and philosophical climate.

In classrooms all over the country there are teachers who were once committed to the ideals of multicultural education but who now feel compelled to deprioritise the issue because of recent changes affecting their practice. Funding for significant projects has long since vanished. Issues of equality have been overtaken in the classroom by issues of assessment, accountability and inspection – all presented as having no relation to stereotyping and race.

Yet racism still exists in all its forms; children remain disadvantaged at all levels of the education system and beyond. 'Rural racism' has evolved into a particular problem. One recent account from a 28 year old manager of a petrol station in Somerset begins:

> I've had racist abuse, robberies threats, knife attacks, you name it... I've had letters telling me to get out within 48 hours or I'll be killed (Brown, 1998 p8).

An exercise conducted in 1996 by the Commission for Racial Equality (CRE) in the North of England using white, Asian, Chinese and black actors demonstrated how racism still plays a part in employment over twenty years after the publication of the Race Relations Act:

> Letters from a black and a white applicant were sent to a well known bank in Glasgow enquiring about vacancies. The white applicant received an application form, while the black applicant was told that there were no suitable openings.
>
> A bakery in Manchester offered interviews to the white and Irish applicants for a trainee post. The black, Asian and Chinese applicants were informed that their applications had been unsuccessful.
>
> A retailer in the Merseyside area informed the black and Asian applicants that the sales vacancy they had applied for had been filled. On the same day, the white, Irish and Chinese applicants received letters inviting them for interviews (CRE, 1997 p2/3).

News reports show that black and Asian people still suffer verbal and physical attacks for no other reason than the colour of their skin, and race clearly remains influential in housing, employment and health. Yet anyone looking at the way we teach our children would have to conclude that learning about the multi-ethnic make-up of Britain is considered irrelevant. If multicultural education ever had a place on the educational agenda it has all but vanished with the advent of the National Curriculum and the current drive towards literacy and numeracy.

Other books chronicle the historical development of multicultural and antiracist education in Britain. Various initiatives and strategies have been initiated and deployed to address the realities: continued racial violence, underachievement by ethnic minority children, exclusion rates and plain ignorance. Each new initiative has attempted to address the issue of racism at some level of society and these issues should be seen within a developing historical and philosophical framework. As this book shows, however, the last twenty years have led to a new plateau of professional indifference. The subject's influence and credibility has deteriorated on at least four levels: political, social, academic, and in relation to teacher training and education.

Whilst the first three are on a wider, national scale, the impact on teacher training is particularly important, not merely because it reflects a growing disinterest in the subject but, crucially, because how our teachers are trained is an indicator of how future generations will be taught. When an issue is effectively removed from the teacher training agenda, it is unreasonable to suppose that it will magically reappear in the classroom practice of newly qualified teachers. The four levels are interrelated and interdependent but we can trace how each has made a particular contribution to the virtual demise of multicultural education and the significant confusion currently experienced by classroom teachers.

1. Political
The political climate of the last twenty years has done little to enhance multicultural education, and there have been overt and deliberate political moves to undermine its credibility in schools. The 1980s began with social uprisings, and an appeal for racial tolerance was made in the Queen's Christmas broadcast of 1982:

> Colour is no longer an indication of national origin. Until this century most racial and religious groups remained concentrated in their homelands but today almost every country of the Commonwealth has become multi-racial and multi-religious. This change has not been without its difficulties, but I believe that for those with a sense of tolerance the arrival and proximity of different races and religions have provided a much better chance for each to appreciate the value of the others (Her Majesty the Queen, cited in AMMA, 1987 p119).

The Swann Report of 1985 identifed racism in the lives of black and Asian children in Britain's schools and sought to point towards solutions at a time of growing racial unrest. In retrospect one can see that its findings were not well received. The Report has had many critics over the years but when it was published it created a new agenda for multicultural education. For the first time in the UK there was a recognisable and concerted effort to go beyond the surface and to deal with issues of prejudice and stereotyping. At the time, its shortcomings were well documented, for example: 'In an astonishing display of insensitivity, dietary requirements or traditions of dress were often simply disregarded' (Finn, 1987).

Although Swann could not be described as radical nor revolutionary, it still stands as the central text pointing to the transition from multicultural education to antiracist education. Its title, 'Education For All' was an indication of intent and, despite some sweeping statements and glaring omissions, there were genuine efforts to represent the needs of all members of society. Whereas early models of governmental dealings with race were based on a policy of non-intervention, the Swann Report was clear in its condemnation:

> All in all, central government appears to have lacked a coherent strategy for fostering the development of multicultural education and thus to have been unable to play a leading role in coordinating or encouraging progress in this field (1985 p220).

Similarly, the Report was prepared to be critical of educators who were still relying on earlier approaches:

> We regard both the assimilationist and integrationist educational responses to the needs of ethnic minority pupils as, in retrospect, misguided and ill-founded (1985 p198).

Perhaps most poignant of all today, the Report was equally scathing about teachers who adopted a 'colour-blind' approach to dealing with the children in their care. A popular claim by teachers at the time (and still to be heard) was that by refusing to acknowledge ethnicity or cultural differences between members of the same class, everyone would be 'treated the same', and equality thus assured. The Report was openly damning of this stance:

> We ... regard 'colour-blindness' ... as potentially just as negative as a straightforward rejection of people with a different skin colour since both types of attitude seek to deny the validity of an important aspect of a person's identity (DES, 1985 pp26-7).

The Commission for Racial Equality has long argued this same point, and made specific references to colour-blindness in their submission to the national commission on education (CRE, 1992 p15). The same point was made repeatedly during the three joint TTA/CRE conferences during 1997, but again no action was taken. The resulting document, *Teaching in Multi-Ethnic Britain* is an action plan for the recruitment and retention of ethnic minority teachers, but the centrally important evidence about colour-blind teaching, and the particular difficulties faced by black students in predominantly white areas of the country were significantly over-looked (Jones, 1997 and 1998a, Lewis, 1997). So it comes as no surprise that the chairman of the CRE has accused the TTA of 'sticking two fingers up at anti-racism' (Ghouri, 1998).

Politically, the concerns of the CRE and others have been marginalised almost out of existence. The Prime Minister openly undermined multicultural education when she stated:

> In the inner cities – where the youngsters must have a decent education if they are to have a better future – that opportunity is all too often snatched from them by hard-left education authorities and extremist teachers. Children who need to be able to count and multiply are learning anti-racist mathematics – whatever that is (Margaret Thatcher reported in Hughill, 1987 p12).

The next Prime Minister said:

> I also want reform of Teacher Training. Let us return to basic subject teaching, not courses in the theory of education. Primary teachers should teach children to read, not waste their time on the politics of gender, race and class (John Major, Speech to the Conservative Party Conference, 1992 cited in Hill, p219).

These statements were not made in political isolation. The New Right was also making multicultural education increasingly impotent on a political level. It had access to and ideological congruence with the government of the day, working on an agenda intended to discredit the views of the Left, presenting them as the champions of lost causes. Thanks to their concerted efforts, egalitarian education, multiculturalism and equality of opportunity became frequent targets. The language of equality and tolerance was countered by the developing notion of 'anti-antiracism', and the concept of equality of opportunity in education was brought into question. It was argued that as a profession, teachers should not waste their time trying to achieve the unachievable by promoting equality of opportunity when so much more effort could be put into a selective process which would yield better results across the board (Wilson, 1991 and 1993). As early as the mid 1980s it was being argued that the New Right was breeding a new kind of racism which 'is all the more pervasive and dangerous precisely because its ideas are not associated with a systematic theory, in that this makes it more difficult to recognise' (Gordon and Klug, 1986 p13). By the end of the decade this movement was matched with undisguised attacks from within the Conservative Party, such the proposal that the DES should issue guidelines to all LEAs to ensure that when dealing with multicultural education they 'should not involve a fostering of ethnic minority cultures, nor a denigration (sic) of Britain's history, heritage or institutions' (Singh and Gill, 1991 p100). Meanwhile, the government was shifting the entire basis for statutory educational provision.

One writer referred to the New Right's conception of education as 'Kentucky Fried Schooling', where schools are run as businesses with the parent as the customer and the pupil as the product (Epstein, 1993 p 24). One MP suggested that schools should aspire to the standards of Marks and Spencers in 'guaranteeing a choice of quality goods served by well trained staff in a disciplined environment under the supervision of strong management' (Jones, 1989 p51). Right wing educationalists were able to sum up their philosophies with statements such as 'Equality in education is as daft as equality in supermarkets. There is no such thing and there is never going to be' (O'Keeffe, 1990 p59).

Just as the New Right were beginning to influence legislation, the last heavily invested multicultural projects were in full flow, evoked by Swann and funded from a wide variety of sources. While the multicultural/antiracist debate was growing more heated, classrooms in selected areas of the country were sites of intense activity in response to involvement in local and national initiatives. One such initiative was the Arts Education for a Multicultural Society (AEMS) project, of which I was an active member. This initiative was designed to place professional black artists in classrooms and try, through the arts, to deal with the race issue at the level of the classroom, working alongside children, teachers, Heads and parents (Jones, 1991, Eggleston, 1995, Robinson and Hustler, 1995). Once an initial two years' funding had ended, schools and project members were encouraged to find their own ways of negotiating more money through the school's own budget or by fundraising activities to maintain the commitment to both the arts and to multiculturalism (I was interested that the commitment to multiculturalism shifted towards antiracism and back again during my time as a project member.) Many member schools did indeed keep up these commitments and some remarkably powerful work was produced by children, but the vast majority of this impetus has undoubtedly been lost over recent years in the drive towards meeting National Curriculum objectives.

2. Social

Issues such as multiculturalism and antiracism had largely disappeared from the public arena by the start of the 1990s. A central tool of the New Right was the appeal for 'plain speaking' and 'common sense', and the dismissal of theoretical debates (such as multiculturalism) as irrelevant and meaningless. As the attack mounted, one could see how multicultural education and antiracism appeared to create arenas where politically motivated activists could grind their own personal axes. For example, at one point in 1993, the interested onlooker had to choose between two parallel protests organised against the rise of the National Front (NF) and the British National Party (BNP) in London (Anderson, 1993). One was conceived and planned by the Anti Nazi League (ANL) and the other by the Anti Racist Alliance (ARA), presenting an immediate dilemma of choice before even beginning to deal with the issues. Then there were protests organised by the Campaign Against Racism and Fascism, Anti Fascist Action, Youth against Racism in Europe, Socialist Action and Red Action amongst others. Each of these groups actively campaigned against the rise of the far Right, but newspaper reports suggest that they spent as much time criticising the agendas of rival antiracist organisations.

Several issues compounded the problem of disunity. One is the form of active resistance supported by each group and the factional political alliances each established. For example, the ANL had the reputation of solid work at ground level organising leafleteers and effective protests, but was also considered as a recruiting organisation for its parent organisation; the Socialist Workers Party. It had a specific focus for its organised confrontation with far Right organisations, but came to be seen increasingly as ineffective when dealing with issues at governmental level and prone to over-exaggeration in its cause. The ARA on the other hand intended to transcend formal political affiliations, but came to be seen as a vehicle for Socialist Action, a splinter group of the Trotskyist International Marxist Group (Mann, 1994a).

In November 1994, antiracist groups were being characterised in the liberal national press as 'riven by personality clashes and factional fighting' (Johnson and Myers, 1994 p4). When Diane Abbott MP was elected chairman of the Anti-Racist Alliance it was expected that some degree of unity would result, and as Britain's largest antiracist group, the ARA would begin to lead by example. Within two weeks, Ms Abbott, three national officers and eleven other executive members had staged a public walk-out and claimed that 'the alliance had squabbled itself out of existence' (Johnson and Myers, 1994). As these fruitless skirmishes increased, the groups whose members were from ethnic minorities became organised and highly visible in areas of racial tension, and adopted changing agendas, leading to warnings of growing militancy amongst young black and Asian people no longer prepared to take abuse passively (Malik, 1995 p7). One report claimed that organised groups from the Bangladeshi populations of Stepney, Poplar and Bethnal Green were not only mistrustful of the police but also increasingly liable to resort to violence in order to defend their communities. As one Youth Connection spokesman claimed:

> We're in a catch 22 situation. You want to defend yourself, but you don't want to go too far. But what is too far? We've tried it non-violently, we've tried everything constructive within the constraints of the law, and it isn't working (Mann,1994b p21).

Police figures on racist incidents have only been kept since 1988, but records since April 1993 indicate that members of ethnic minorities were up to four times more likely to be stopped and questioned, and that in court they are more likely to be charged than cautioned (Travis, 1995). Other statistics of the time indicated that Afro-Caribbean boys were four times more likely to be expelled than their white peers, and twice as likely to face unemployment (Younge, 1995). The annual number of racial incidents continued to rise at a rate of 13 per cent a year (Klein, 1995a), and racially motivated attacks tripled in Tower Hamlets during the weeks following the BNP's success in electing a far-Right candidate to power (Mann, 1994b).

The Stephen Lawrence and Michael Menson cases illustrate that racism continues to be a violent issue (Gentleman, 1998, Pallister 1998 a and b). More recent statistics suggests we are still waiting for improvement, for example the current exclusion rate amongst Afro-Caribbean boys remains unchanged (Ghouri and Barnard, 1999), and other reports suggest that in some part of the country these children are now 15 times more likely to be expelled than their white counterparts (Ousley, 1998, Phillips, 1998, Thornton 1998). While this chapter was being written two local accounts of racial violence were reported on the radio: a young Asian man was kicked to death in a fish and chip shop, and an Asian taxi driver was attacked but returned with twenty friends to beat his oppressors. It is worth noting that Helen's school, discussed later in the book, is situated in the area where these attacks took place. As racially motivated violence continues to escalate across Europe it seems remarkable that there is no popular, coordinated voice seeking to undermine the rise of the far Right and further the cause of antiracism.

From a teacher's point of view, the plethora of news reports, the rhetoric of the New Right and the weight of public opinion meant that multicultural education became a potentially dangerous issue to promote, particularly in all-white primary schools. The introduction and ongoing development of the National Curriculum took clear precedence over any multicultural initiatives, and teachers who would have liked to incorporate multicultural ideals in their practice found themselves buried beneath the weight of educational legislation and parental pressure to achieve within the stated guidelines.

Whilst initiatives such as the AEMS project had demonstrated that there were productive ways of dealing with race in the predominantly white classroom, there was a parallel retreat away from the issue at national level. A multicultural task group was set up by the National Curriculum Council (NCC) in July 1989 in response to a letter from the secretary of state for education some eleven months earlier, instructing the NCC to 'take account of ethnic and cultural diversity for all pupils regardless of ethnic origin or gender' (cited in Tomlinson, 1993 p21). £49,000 had been set aside for the publication of multicultural guidance from the resulting nine months work by the NCC but it never saw the light of day. Tomlinson describes how executive officers at the NCC, DES officials and politicians fought for control of the document, leaving black pressure groups, academics and practitioners completely outside the debate, and concludes that there were two reasons why the report was never published. Firstly, both multicultural and anti-racist education were perceived to be part of a hard Left tendency that wanted to infiltrate the education system and, secondly, significant Right wing pressure groups had successfully urged the promotion and maintenance of British culture (sic) (Tomlinson, 1993 p25).

Others have argued that the Education Reform Act was the culmination of the previous government's desire to control the education system for political gain. In the late 1980s it was argued that the ERA was 'an important weapon in the ideological arsenal of the Thatcher government' (Ball and Troyna, 1989 p24), its ideology representing a free market philosophy, extolling the virtues of competition, privatisation and efficiency. Others argued that the National Curriculum reflected the ethnocentric view of the ruling class and was an example of the New Right's idea of nationalism (Menter, 1992 p6). It was further argued that the ERA and National Curriculum could only be inegalitarian because its design was ideologically rooted in the notion of competitive individualism (Ball and Troyna, 1989 p27) and it was recognised that the National Curriculum would certainly result in fewer opportunities for multiculturalists and antiracists to operate:

> Hitherto ... the structural decentralisation of the education system in England and Wales has permitted a degree of autonomy at the local level. It is within this 'space' that campaigns for racial equality in education have been waged, albeit with different degrees of commitment and vigour ... The ERA will almost certainly deny this 'space', a prospect which has deleterious implications for the promotion of anti-racism (Ball and Troyna, 1989 p24).

At the wider social level there has been an equally negative effect on the cause of multicultural education. Language seems to have become as much a part of the developing conflict within the issue as either political ideology or passionate belief. As the shifts in linguistic terms became more pronounced and more divisive, the interested parties began to fracture alongside the argument, resulting in further disunity and antagonism. The drive towards definition of the issue seems to have been matched only by the desire to control it. The various pressure groups and parties that champion the issues of antiracism and multiculturalism have begun to multiply to the point where their message is becoming partial and little more that a justification of their own existence.

3. Academic

Here the role of the teacher must be kept centre stage. How do the debates impact on professional understanding and influence class-room practice? That said, disintegration of the subject appears to have taken place at an academic as well as a social level, leaving multicultural education conceptually, practically and ideologically adrift of classroom practice.

By the end of the 1980s, the teacher or student entering teaching would encounter two main schools of thought along a philosophical and ideological continuum. Much of the contention surrounding the two polar positions can be related back to the Swann Report, but the added dimension in the 1990s was the enforced National Curriculum which ordered content knowledge to be taught across Key Stages. Of course the National Curriculum had the potential to bring some of the Swann Report's recommendations to bear in schools, but instead it provided further confusion for the practi-tioner and more power to multicultural education's opponents.

At one end of the continuum were the traditional multiculturalists who wanted to respond to the Swann Report by working at grass roots level to promote equality of opportunity and racial harmony through a variety of initiatives. By then many traditional multiculturalists were becoming fearful that an acceptance of multiculturalism would only lead to being branded as tokenistic, liberal and dealing in cultural exotica (Taylor, 1990 p373), but they were unwilling to embrace what they perceived to be hard line antiracism which (apparently) demanded nothing less than social revolution. They could argue that they had adjusted their multicultural position to deal with racism, but were always faced with the antiracist argument that the two positions are 'irreconcilable concepts of educational change' (Troyna, 1987 p307). Small wonder that many multiculturalists became prepared to sidestep the debate completely rather than find themselves trapped in this ideological struggle, and opted for 'doing nothing'.

In the retreat from accusations of meaningless white liberalism, some multiculturalists found solace in small scale initiatives, which reveal a confused movement desperately wanting to avoid the 'doing good by doing little' syndrome, but unsure about what actually needed to be done. Some were still discussing ideas about twinning predominantly white schools with multi-ethnic inner city schools, suggesting that the 'cultural diversity' approach was still valid as long as it recognised the existence of racism and as long as teachers were prepared to challenge racism when it occurred in the classroom (Brown *et al*, 1990 pp3-12, Hix, 1992 p4). Others claimed that the situation was improving because the trend in children's literature had moved away from 'fake multiculturalism' and 'unreadable, pretentious writing' as written by white writers in the 1970s and early 1980s and towards a 'genuinely multicultural contribution to children's literature' (Eccleshare, 1991 p23) by publishing more black writers. Other local initiatives that received wider attention included a study that recommended that children begin to evaluate the forms of bias and stereotype found in their school library books (Goodwin and Wellings, 1992), and the historical 'building blocks' project to encourage children to value their own languages and recognise that their own experiences and stories form a subjective view of the past (Hazareesingh, 1993).

Multiculturalists who attempted to breach the gulf between the two extremes also seemed doomed. In attempting to establish the 'common framework of values' first suggested by the Swann Report this aim was naively presumed to be a commonly held goal, and consequently the recommendations made (Lynch, 1987 pp1-15 and Leicester, 1989 pp32-4) remained heavily reliant on a perceived form of democracy that had, by the early 1990s, disappeared in educational terms. Most multiculturalists were keen to challenge racism in the classroom and to explore school texts for bias and stereotypes, but this was clearly insufficient for the antiracist lobbies. One writer identified the situation at the end of the 1980s as a conflict between 'left antiracism', which he identified as relying primarily on structural theory and a class analysis of education, and 'new multiculturalism' which he claimed was little more than old multiculturalism plus the recognition of institutional racism (Hatcher, 1987 p184). Whilst the distinctions made between the two stances are interesting and confirm their incompatibility, little suggests a route forward. Hatcher called for 'alliances for change' between the teaching profession, black communities and the Labour Party to ensure that antiracist principles were not compromised:

> The task now facing the movement for antiracist education is to continue to construct a growing web of connections at school, local, and national levels, between what happens in classrooms and the wider political struggles outside, in the form of not only campaigns to implement or defend specific reforms, but also of a comprehensive programme for antiracist education in schools around which unity can be built among the social forces capable of installing it (Hatcher, 1987 p199).

This call to arms was met with silence and the relationship between multiculturalism and antiracism has since deteriorated to the point where such an alliance now seems highly improbable. There remains large-scale suspicion of antiracist education. 'Antiracist education, at least in all-white areas, has been aborted' (Patel, 1994 p227). Ethnic minority groups have criticised antiracism as a detraction from the white mainstream, qualification-focused education that leads to success (Weston 1989a), and teachers' unions have criticised antiracism as creating further racial tensions in multicultural schools (Weston, 1989b) and resisted the recommendations of the Lawrence Inquiry (Macpherson, 1999), asserting indignantly that their members are not racist (Richardson, 1999). Multiculturalists, too, criticised antiracist education, echoing the claim that:

> ...so-called anti-racist education is likely to be either not education at all but anti-racist propaganda, or is in substance little different from multicultural education (Parekh, 1986 p30).

This was precisely the stance that Troyna and Williams identified earlier as deracialised discourse (Troyna and Williams, 1986), indicating that multiculturalism had become part of a slogan system, a political and linguistic reconceptualisation that relied more heavily on the management of local specific issues related primarily to black pupils, rather than trying to deal with the root causes of racism in society. The central problem was that multiculturalists did not want to deal with racism on this level, were keen to disassociate themselves from views that proposed radical and revolutionary change and were quick to point out that 'A major problem confronting antiracists is the absence of consensus on precisely what should be fought' (Jeffcoate, 1985 p61). There were accusations that antiracism was threatening to teacher autonomy, undermining the education system's desired impartiality with ideological indoctrination and totalitarianism. Antiracism was no longer a popular liberal concept based on equality and justice, appealing to teachers across the country at grass roots level, but instead seen as a political tool in the hands of the few who promoted revolutionary agendas.

The response for some multiculturalists was to return to the supposed impartiality of the school and the professionalism of teachers: much as we might abhor certain examples of stereotyping and 'racism in the original sense' (sic), 'our job is not to combat opinions we do not like but to uphold democratic principles and procedures' (Jeffcoate, 1985 p62). It is easy with hindsight to see that this ideological equivalent of burying one's head in the sand was exactly what allowed the government to ignore democratic principles and procedures and to introduce legislation to ensure that opinions they did not like were discredited or outlawed. The ostrich strategy has surely helped to create a system where:

> The education offered to black and Asian children does not equip them to deal with the experience of racism and the world as they perceive it. That education is equally irrelevant to white children (Matthews, 1992 p35).

At the other end of the continuum, the antiracist lobby claimed that the Swann Report was responsible for the current crisis because it failed to articulate the dimensions of institutional and structural racism. Certain writers claim that all of Swann's work is rendered invalid because it reduces the 'problem' to a comfortable liberal issue which reinforces weak multiculturalism, pluralism or even re-generates the ghosts of assimilationism and integrationism:

> Swann's understanding of nation and ethnicity, with its repeated emphasis on stability, cohesion and common identity, is one that ignores structural divisions and conflicts of interest between different groups. This means that racism is primarily presented as individual prejudice, based on negative cultural stereotypes (Carter and Williams, 1987 p 172).

The insistence that racism be defined as wider than individual prejudice has continued to be a central theme of the antiracist lobby, who accordingly dismiss not only multicultural initiatives but also other antiracist initiatives that used a weakened definition:

> The racialized education policies of the 1980s amounted to little more than an exercise in left-wing gesture politics. Despite the move towards racialization, antiracist education policies, like the more radical multi-cultural policies, contrived a version of reality in which racism was seen as independent of and not integral to the way society is organized, struc-tured and legitimated (Troyna, 1993 p42).

These authors speak for those who felt that educationalists needed to realise that it was only through a radical reappraisal of societal structures and concerted change at all levels of society that racism would begin to change.

The stalemate throughout the 1990s has been palpable, leaving many to abandon their commitment to multicultural ideals or to rely on the language of 'good practice' and models of permeation.

Yet schools are not all impotent within the multicultural equation. Although they cannot alter economic and social structures they can certainly make a difference to children's lives. Although schools cannot eradicate racism, they can challenge it, deal with racist material and the growth of racist ideas amongst the school population. Parekh also argued thus, stating that:

> ...the school can hope to undercut the intellectual and moral roots of racism and weaken it. It cannot, of course, hope to eliminate it altogether, for education has its limits and the social and political roots of racism lie beyond the control of the school. However it can make its significant contribution by tackling the intellectual and moral basis of racism that is amenable to and indeed falls within its purview. To ask it to do more is perhaps the surest way to ensure that it will not be able to do even this much (Parekh, 1986 p31).

Here lies much of the solution. Primary schools in particular are built on the relationships between teachers and pupils and the belief that these relationships can bring about significant change to the lives of young people. If not, our collective concept of the education of young people needs to be drastically reworked. Multicultural research in multi-ethnic schools in Manchester and London confirms this view, concluding that much of the good and bad work being done was a direct result of the quality of relationships within each institution (Verma, Zec and Skinner, 1994). Similar relationships were built out of the AEMS Project (Jones 1991, 1998), leading me to believe that success can be translatable from the multi-ethnic school to the exclusively or predominantly white school. If this is to happen, then significant responsibility lies with those who train our teachers.

4. Teacher training and education

Teacher training must therefore play a large part in determining the future of multicultural and antiracist education, and the four research 'stories' which follow are vital indicators of what needs to be done. The context for these stories is the discrepancy between the form and content of initial teacher education and its relationship with multicultural education, especially in predominantly white regions of the country. If effective teaching stems from sensitive and professional relationships in educational contexts, standards can hardly be expected to improve through the imposition of a knowledge-based curriculum and the reduction of teachers to mechanistic transmitters of information. If effective learning concerning race-related issues stems also from the strength of the relationship between the teacher, the institution and the learner, the first question must be 'How are these relationships acquired?' Are they the result of personal qualities that are merely enhanced as the beginning teacher learns his or her craft, are they learnt *in situ*, acquired by osmosis from crafted practitioners? Or are they definable skills that can be taught and learnt? In which case, how far are training institutions aware of the power of these relationships and to what extent are beginning teachers being encouraged to create and nurture learning relationships?

The fostering of these relationships is problematic however, because of the politicised nature of education and of initial teacher training. The pressure on schools to succeed in a competitive market place keeps rising. Teachers have had to manage the National Curriculum, Ofsted inspections, league tables, parental onslaughts and other unimagined professional challenges. There was little space for multicultural education, particularly in white areas, as schools prioritised their needs and planned accordingly. The current drive towards literacy and numeracy hours is likely to compound this further, leaving multicultural and antiracist education further than ever from the chalk face of the predominantly white classrooms identified by Swann as the places where the need is greatest.

Just as schools have had to contend with the enormous pace of change, universities and institutions of teacher training across the country have found their curricula tightened in order to meet specific training criteria laid down by the DfEE. Many of the courses and modules which aimed to establish professional, creative and supportive relationships between teachers and learners have been lost as the weight of training passes into the school and students are expected to learn 'on the job', as part of a 'partnership' process. Much of the space for understanding childhood, for personal reflection and for critical understanding has been replaced with lectures in how to transmit knowledge. This simplistic transmission-based form of education holds all kinds of implications for teachers currently being trained. The remainder of this book explores what this means at the level of the classroom, and sets out to locate areas where multicultural education might have been particularly appropriate and to identify ways forward.

Chapter 2
The Research Project

The students I chose to study came from two separate institutions of initial teacher education and were enrolled on primary PGCE courses. Between the two institutions, the training offered experience over three counties using schools where virtually all the children were white. The formal training offered no contact with ethnic minority teachers, mentors or lecturers. One institution was able to offer teaching attachments in a small number of inner city schools but this affected only two of my sample group, the typical experience for the majority of students on both courses being rural or semi-rural. The students arrived with degrees in a variety of subjects, they had had varying amounts of pre-course contact with children and came from a range of socio-economic backgrounds. Lest it appear that I selected an exclusively white sample for the purposes of this study, it should be noted that the entire intake of PGCE Key Stage Two students in both institutions had not a single member from any ethnic minority group. The particular problems of recruiting black people to PGCE courses have already been documented (Siraj-Blatchford, 1991 and 1993), and this is compounded in predominantly (if not exclusively) white localities.

One institution had evolved its training into a school-based model, the other was university-based but moving into school-based partnerships. To collect my data I examined course documentation and interviewed course leaders and tutors, Heads, supervisory teachers, mentors and the students themselves. I built participant observation into the research design and obtained permission to attend relevant lectures, workshops and field trips which included two visits to a Mosque, visits to two Sikh temples, a 'multicultural day' and an equal opportunities session.

In all, a total of 55 (23 faculty-based and 32 school-based) students arrived on the two courses and I arranged to meet all who were willing to take part in my study in small, informal groups during their induction week. At the school-based university, 25 agreed to take part in initial interviews. On the university-based course 17 of the 23 course members agreed to an initial interview, but only 16 kept their appointments. At these initial meetings I explained that I was interested in studying their experiences as beginning teachers and that I would narrow this down to a smaller number to monitor over the coming year. I asked some general questions about their geographical backgrounds and expectations of the course, and asked them to do a brief but formal rank order exercise on their responses to aspects of teacher training/ education that they felt were most and least valuable at this point in their understanding. There followed a broad discussion about their perceptions about educational inequality and the potential for social differences between groups of children. Each small group meeting was taped, and as I had given each student a number in my notes and monitored the sequence of speakers, the tapes helped me to identify the individual contributors to the discussions.

Over the following week I selected and contacted ten students from each institution to constitute my working sample groups. My selection was made according to several conscious decisions. All 25 students I interviewed on the school-based course offered to commit themselves to further study and I then looked for a variety of social backgrounds and pre-course experience, and examined their contributions to the group discussions. I would opt for those who seemed happy to contribute their ideas in an open forum, and I was also influenced by any race-related issues that arose out of the conversations, or if they expressed ideas about disadvantage or inequality that might be potential starting points for later discussions. Only ten of the original sixteen on the university-based course who attended the initial group meetings offered to be part of the sample group, so my selection was made for me.

I arranged to interview each student formally at three stages over the course of their training and several other unplanned, opportunistic interviews were also conducted. The first interviews were to be as soon as possible after their induction week and would provide more detail into their insights, personal beliefs and their course expectations. The second interviews would be based in schools at an agreed mid-point in their training, so I could contextualise their discussions about their progress in light of the location and 'quality' of their training and experience. This would also facilitate supplementary interviews with their Headteachers, supervising teachers and mentors. The final interviews were scheduled for a convenient time in the last two weeks of the course in order to gather final reflections and impressions. While this structure seemed quite instinctive, its physical arrangement presented some organisational difficulties. Whereas I had imagined that the first round of interviews would be the simplest of all, and that the university itself would be the location, this was not the case. The structure of the school-based course meant that the beginning teachers had a brief introductory series of lectures and were then sent out into schools almost immediately on an initial four week Key Stage One school attachment. My sample group were therefore scattered around three counties and more difficult to locate, but it seemed too good an opportunity to miss as they would already have more to discuss in terms of their first hand experience in schools. Accordingly, I arranged to conduct my first round of interviews with these students in their observation schools.

As the second round of interviews for all students was to take place in schools I used the opportunity to include some participant observation. I made myself available to all members of both sample groups, offering to team teach alongside them or to act as their classroom assistant for the day. I felt that I would be able to familiarise myself more intimately with the students, staff, children and the internal dynamics of their schools, and that it would be more productive to hold the interview at the end of a school day in which I had taken a meaningful, professional role. My offer was typical of what has been called a 'helping relationship' (Delamont, 1992 p135) or 'favor-bank' (Fine and Deegan, 1996 p440), whereby services are offered in order to create a sense of obligation on the part of the respondent to return as much goodwill (in this instance in the form of interviews) as possible.

The final round of interviews took place, as scheduled, during the last two weeks of the course. The school-based students were still in their partner schools at the end of their course, so I could see them at the end of their school day, but it was more problematic with the university-based students. The final section of their course consisted mainly of compulsory formal lectures based in the university. Although they were all in one location, they were working to a heavy timetable that they later described as frustrating, time-consuming and irrelevant to their qualification, and for some the prospect of an interview after one such day was not particularly welcome.

The first round of interviews took the form of semi-structured, open-ended questioning, usually based around not only race but also areas of their own education and social backgrounds, their reasons for entering the profession, their pre-course school experiences and their early experiences of the course in general. It quickly became apparent during my data collection that unless the interviews were widened to include more personal experiences in schools, the students would feel that I was not trying to understand their real feelings about the course and would become defensive over the issue of race because there was so little to discuss. Once I had established some idea about the subject's understanding about race or ethnicity the situation quickly became difficult to negotiate as the issue was not part of their training in the university nor their experience in school, and so the more I pressed for answers the less I felt I was likely to find out, as the respondent retreated into a defensive position.

The second round of interviews, which took place in Key Stage Two classrooms, were again semi-structured, using open-ended questions focused more on the school situation, predominantly the student's experiences with the children and the quality of provision offered by the supervising teacher/mentor. Again, however, the race issue seemed irrelevant to their experiences and discussions around the subject remained rather limited. Often students would say that they had already given me the answer during the first round of interviews, and they seemed confused about why I was insistent upon travelling into such a philosophical cul-de-sac.

The final interviews were slightly more formal in that I worked to a more structured list of questions and could return to specific statements the students had made at different points over the year to see how their perceptions had changed in the light of their training and school experience. Here I could return more naturally to their initial statements about race, gender, social class, disadvantage and educational inequality and then explore how those perceptions had developed.

All interviews were taped, transcribed in full and returned to the students for formal validation. When transcribing the interviews, pauses were represented by '...', significantly longer pauses were represented by '(silence)'. Any heavy emphasis on a single word or short phrase used by the respondent was represented in italics in the transcription. There were occasions when, particularly in the third series of interviews, sensitive issues were discussed that the respondent requested be left out of the transcription. I complied fully with any such requests, representing these with '(omission)' in the transcript. None of this evidence has been accessed for the purposes of this book.

Understandably, the students I traced did not seem to be interested in my research at any level as they were (quite rightly) engrossed in their course. They were often flattered to have been chosen (for some reason imperceptible to them), but did not want to know the details of the study. Their understanding of my interventions into their training was that I was studying them because I was in some way interested in initial teacher education and they seemed happy to accept that this was perfectly natural. I suspected that the race issue seemed to be an almost irrelevant by-product of this process for many of them, and this was borne out when, at the end of my final interviews, I asked what my research had been about. Every sample group student referred to the issues of school-based training, only two mentioned multiculturalism and/or equal opportunities, one thought I had been studying gender issues and another said she had no idea at all and asked me outright to explain what I had been studying.

My interviews with Heads, course leaders, teachers, mentors and university lecturers were quite different in character, and many subjects were keen to understand the precise nature of my study and how I had arrived at this point from the position of being a classroom practitioner. Their responses were typically more detailed and carefully considered in the light of professional experience. All bar one of the interviews with lecturers were taped (one insisted that I only make handwritten notes). Interviews with mentors and supervising teachers were usually taped, but typically these respondents were not interested in transcripts of our conversations, neither did they want to get involved in any aspect of the validation process even though this was offered. Several respondents felt that they were prepared to find time in their schedules to talk to me in an interview context, but simply did not want to 'waste' time authenticating transcripts. One key respondent told me that she only wanted to read any parts of the transcript that contained 'anything incriminating', leaving me to decide what might fall into that category. In some cases school-based respondents were happier not to be taped at all but for me to take notes and repeat key statements to them at the end of the interview to make sure I had understood their feelings correctly and that my notes were accurate. In two cases, small groups of teachers or mentors said that they felt more comfortable being interviewed together as it allowed them to be more honest with me, knowing that nothing could be directly ascribed to them at a personal level. In these cases I agreed to ascribe all responses to a single respondent under an invented name.

From within the sample group I also selected four students, two from each university, to study in greater depth as potential life studies. Rather than pretend that each would somehow represent a generalisable aspect of wider ITE or race awareness, I hoped that the broader, more subtle and sensitive data generated by this smaller group would provide a contextualising framework within which I could locate the specific experiences of four young people and the way they managed their transition from graduate student to professional educator. This process involved interviewing at greater length, depth and frequency, arranging further interviews at the university and in school contexts so as to experience the full range of provision offered to the student. Where these students had more than one school placement or were offered experience with a different class of children I made every effort to take these shifts into account. The decision to develop four of my sample group as life studies also allowed me to arrange further meetings and interviews wherever possible with all the teachers responsible for that student's classroom practice so as to gain maximum linked insights into the character of their school and university experiences. As with the sample group interviews, all life study interviews throughout the year were transcribed in full and returned to the student for validation.

In total, this meant that I conducted 157 formal interviews. Of these, 107 took place with students, 32 with supervising teachers, mentors and Heads and 18 with university staff. I visited 24 schools in three counties over the year, some in the role as researcher/observer, some in the role of teacher/subject expert/ classroom assistant. In each school I visited I had some contact with the supervising teacher/mentor, although the quality and time differed enormously. In each school I also asked to see relevant documentation related to multicultural education and made field notes with particular reference to displays, ethnic minority population, staffroom notices and library provision.

The four stories I have chosen here are largely because the experiences of these beginning teachers highlighted one or more of the issues I set out to study. These four stories are not presented as typical or representative of wider student experiences on all primary PGCE courses. Rather, the experiences of these four students characterise a time when issues of social justice are fading from the agenda, and when school-based training is becoming the predominant model for ITE.

No male students are represented in this analysis, simply because of the four male beginning teachers selected for my sample, three withdrew at various stages (one after failing his final school attachment), while the fourth passed the course but did not respond to my call for the final round of interviews. All the female students passed their course and maintained their full commitment to my research.

All respondents and children have been given pseudonyms to protect anonymity and confidentiality. Similarly, 'Midshire' is used to disguise the precise locations of the ITE institutions and the participating schools.

Chapter 3

Helen's Story

Race and professional discourses

Witness

Although Helen was one of my original sample group, she was not selected as a case study but throughout her course I had far more contact with her than any other student in my core sample. She had recently married and instead of taking up nursing, had entered the course as a mature student. Helen was one of the students who accepted my offer to work in the classroom during my second round of interviews and I spent time with her Y3 class working on a combined history/design and technology/art project, along with her mentor and a parent helper. The school was one of only three urban institutions in my sample and the only one that had any substantial numbers of ethnic minority children, three of whom were in Helen's class. There was no indication that I had entered the school on a multicultural agenda. As far as anyone knew, I was there to see how the business of partnership and mentor training was working for initial teacher education.

My time working in Helen's classroom passed productively, the children were well motivated, relationships between the children and adults in the room appeared to be a warm and I saw nothing which I would have categorised as 'negative'. I thoroughly enjoyed working with the children, who responded well to Helen's teaching, and I felt that their end products were the results of some real collaborative learning. Helen and I were due to meet for an interview at the end of a school day, after I had interviewed her mentor half an hour earlier, leaving her space to pull together the day's activities and draw some preliminary conclusions with the children. Just beforehand, I set up my tape recorder in preparation for both interviews in a photocopying room which was not being used. I then came back to the classroom where Helen was concluding the activities and, not wanting to interrupt her, stood outside the door, waiting for the teacher to return and listening to Helen praise the children for their efforts.

While I waited, some forty or so older children began filing out of the school hall, making their way back to their classrooms. There was no sign of a teacher. I noted that every child had a magenta dot on their forehead and there was obvious discomfort. Two or three of the children were visibly of ethnic minority origin. I noticed that some of the white boys in particular were walking hurriedly with their faces down, clearly embarrassed. Two boys from another class, about two years younger, stood laughing at them in the doorway to my left.

Although the children leaving the hall could see me clearly, neither of the younger boys realised that I was only inches away from them on the other side of the door frame. They shrieked, pointed and one chanted: 'Pakis! Pakis!' to which the second added: 'Look at them, they're trying to be Pakis!' The first went on loudly: 'I bet they've been making curry all afternoon'. The class shuffled on silently, ignoring the taunts and as they passed I realised that an Asian girl had stopped and was staring at the two boys. She was shaking with anger and once the class passed she was left facing them alone. There was still no sign of a teacher. The boys by this time were howling with laughter and pointing directly at the girl. She was now shaking so much that I couldn't tell whether she was about to attack them or burst into tears.

As I stepped out of the doorway the boys registered my presence, looked at me, turned, and ran back into their own classroom. When I went to speak to the girl she ran in the opposite direction, following her classmates. From my right, Helen's mentor appeared for our appointed interview. The corridor was empty and we moved into the photocopying room to talk.

This moment still haunts me. As a teacher, all my instincts were to deal with the incident immediately, but I had been told only days earlier that I needed to take a more 'scientifically detached' approach to my research, distancing myself as far as possible from the object of my study in order to maintain validity, and I felt as though my intervention would in some way invalidate or taint the data collection. It took another year of heated debate with my supervisory team to overcome this methodological hurdle, but this is of no comfort to the Asian girl (for a full account see Jones 1998b). At the time, and to my shame, I let confusion reign and took the easier option of following the mentor back into the photocopying room and starting the interview, hoping to gain some insight into the institutional context in which the abuse had taken place.

Helen's mentor had spent her entire career in the same school. She told me that she had received no training before being asked to supervise students. She said that when she came to the school there were no ethnic minority children: 'Well, let's say that when I came 32 years ago we had one little West Indian boy who used to sit in the nursery and cry because: 'Why wasn't anybody like... he was?'. She told me that just after the war the two schools in the area used to be considered part of a residential district which was 'quite elite', but that now more Asian families had moved in. Fewer had moved into the area immediately adjacent to the school because the houses: 'are more your two up two down and the bathroom conversion at the back. They are not the larger houses that the Asian people go for'. She stated that there was no multicultural policy or statement in the school, but that they were: 'looking towards writing one'. The school was, she said, a 'happy' one.

All through the interview with Helen's mentor I was conscious that there were questions I did not know how to ask, and I was convinced that I needed a reason to return to the school as soon as possible with a carefully considered plan to explore the incident further. Coincidentally, when I went back to the classroom to interview Helen, her mother and husband had paid a surprise visit and she asked if we could postpone our meeting. I willingly agreed and asked if it would be possible to arrange a short interview with the Head at that visit. I decided to write a 'fictional' account of the incident and follow my semi-structured outline interview plan when I returned to the school, but then introduce the 'story' of a child being attacked in the corridor and ask people in the school how they thought such an incident might be tackled. I felt that this strategy would give me an agenda to question the school about their own procedures without necessarily putting them on the defensive from the onset. Secondly, it gave me the chance to explore Helen's perceptions of the issue and, finally, to find out whether anything had happened during my absence as I knew that some forty children had witnessed the incident.

I still felt extremely vulnerable as a researcher. I knew of no other examples of the approach I was planning and felt that I was moving into dangerous territory open to all kinds of criticisms about researcher objectivity. My only certainty was that this was the first time that race had been a real issue during my tour of the 'white highlands' and that it needed to be aired if I was to understand the incident within its educational context. After taking this stance I came across a number of similar strategies, and began to believe that there was merit in using data to provoke more data.

One study in particular helped me forward. A group of researchers were witness to a racial attack in a predominantly white primary school in Scotland. In this instance a de-racialised, 'fictional' account of a racial attack at a birthday party was retold to the children involved and their peers, who all interpreted the incident as unfair, nasty and clearly the result of jealousy. When the children were given a photograph of a white girl and told that this was the victim, their interpretations of the incident were confirmed. When they were presented with a photograph of an Asian girl and told that she had been the victim (as had been the case in reality), their responses changed dramatically: 'Without exception, the pupils changed their theory about the motivation for the attack. The jealous theory was discarded. 'Oh', they now said, 'it's because she's black' (Donald et al., 1995 p270).

While I would like to claim that published accounts such as this motivated my developing methodology, I have to admit that at the time I was simply trying to find some better way of understanding.

My method was nowhere near as well conceived as in the account above but my intentions were similar. I constructed a faithful, fictional prose account of the incident I had witnessed so as to provoke responses in a context which, at the time of the telling, were unlikely to be seen as a personal or professional accusation.

When I returned to the school to meet Helen, the interview was relaxed and warm. She had had a change of partner schools after a difficult experience and wanted very much to tell me how positive she now felt, how supportive she found the school and how the university had been able to identify a potentially damaging relationship and set wheels into motion to remedy the situation. In the time between my two visits, Helen's university had provided an equal opportunities session which I had attended (and which is discussed in Rachel's story). When we moved on to the subject of equality of opportunity she said that she found that the discussion of race and multicultural issues at the university:

> ...didn't tell me anything I didn't already know. I think if you are already sensitive to the issues then (pause) you know, you are preaching to the converted really.

I asked if she felt challenged in any way by the issues raised. She replied that she had felt only that it was 'a little bit patronising at times'.

This session at the university was not the first time that Helen had encountered the issue of race. In her first school experience – at another school in the same area – we had discussed multicultural policies and Helen told me that:

> They have got an equal opportunities policy, it's racism they haven't got a policy about (pause). One member of staff thought that there ought to be a policy on racism, but there were some that were against that because they thought that by having a policy it meant that you would be talking to the children about it and it would bring a contentious topic to the fore when before it wasn't surfacing. But 'Paki' and things had been bandied about and this member of staff said she felt there was a need for it, but there was resistance (pause) they think that by discussing it they would create a problem that wasn't there before.

Remembering this, I asked whether there was a multicultural policy in Helen's current school. She replied that she had asked for it and that there wasn't one, elaborating:

> I asked if there was racial tension and she (the Head) said 'We very much deal with them as and when they come up' and 'We speak to the parents...' sort of things like that.

This was confirmed when I later interviewed the Head, who told me that there was no multicultural policy in the school, that there was no agreed method of dealing with racial incidents and that the school was not really 'party to these things'.

> No, I haven't got one, and I don't think we (pause) I don't think (pause) it is one of the many policies that I haven't got and we should have. I think that equal opportunities covers that.

While the lack of a formal equal opportunities policy or multicultural education policy does not, in itself, equate with an absence of commitment, the lack of documentation in this case coupled with the incident I had witnessed and the statements made by staff in interview led me to believe that equal opportunities was not a strong feature of the school. This is not uncommon, and in my research I found virtually no evidence of any formal commitment to equality issues, even when a member of staff insisted that the school was sensitive to such issues.

The Macdonald Inquiry into Burnage School was one of many studies that have highlighted the problematic relationship between the rhetoric of multicultural and antiracist policies and the reality of implementation and practice. Typical findings were: 'It is clear that any antiracist policy... will be totally ineffective if carried out in a vacuum' (Macdonald *et al*, 1989 p351) and that policies which have been 'grafted-on' can 'easily lead to a marginalisation' whereby non-involved staff are able to see themselves as exempt from responsibility for dealing with these issues (p386).

At a time when OFSTED inspectors appear to have heeded earlier criticisms that they had neglected equality issues (Pyke, 1995a), and are now making overt reports on the quality of equal opportunities provision, the fact that some schools have not even begun to address the issue ought to be a matter for concern. Their Report on the attainment of minority ethnic pupils (OFSTED, 1999) now requires all schools to monitor attainment by ethnicity, to record racist incidents and to have and implement policies on race equality.

The existence of a multicultural statement or policy became something of an issue during the course of my data collection. Both course leaders seemed to presume that the requirement on beginning teachers to collect relevant school information would include these documents, but whenever I asked for details about equal opportunities or multicultural policies and statements students would invariably give me answers such as:

> They don't need an equal opps policy here, it's an all female staff.

> I didn't notice multicultural or equal opps policies. They seem to be kind of Christian oriented.

> I shouldn't think there's a multicultural statement to be honest but I'll ask.

> It is being drawn up at the moment.

> There is no multicultural policy as such. It's coming through on the RE because that's what the school inspector insisted.

> They are trying to get them reeled off at the moment for the OFSTED.

It would be easy to dismiss these responses as merely those of unmotivated students unlikely to locate documentary evidence which they perceived as neither overtly requested by the university nor of real importance in an all-white primary school. It is scarcely surprising. As one Headteacher wrote:

> Any course about multicultural education tends to be greeted in Cornwall by a mixture of amazement and amusement. When... I attended a 25 day course organised by Exeter University, my staff could hardly contain their mirth (Whalley, 1987 p67).

The problem becomes compounded, however, when we add the reluctance to address the issue by Helen's Headteacher and responses to the same request that other Heads, class teachers and mentors gave me:

> I don't know if there is a policy or not to be honest. I think we've got a policy for just about everything. It must be in something somewhere. I

> don't know. Don't quote me on that. Ask me about special needs (Mentor on school-based PGCE course).
>
> We are looking towards writing a multicultural education policy (Head-teacher on school-based PGCE course).
>
> There is a draft equal opps policy and we have a separate multicultural education policy. I know there is one but when I asked to see it the Head said he had lost it (Mentor on school-based PGCE course).

During my year of data collection I could locate only one multicultural education policy and this was sent to me by a student from a school that was not part of my sample group. This suggests that either schools genuinely did not have any such documentation available for scrutiny, if they did they were not prepared (for whatever reason) to let outsiders such as myself and the beginning teachers have access to it, or that the documentation was in a state of flux so the school felt reluctant to offer it for scrutiny until it was in some finalised form. Whatever the reality, it is clear that multicultural education was, for these schools, certainly not an issue which had great impact on the curriculum they provided, nor was it a focal point for intended dialogue between school supervisors and beginning teachers.

When I presented Helen with my 'fictional' story I asked what she thought would happen if the incident had occurred in her school. She told me:

> Well I would expect that both parties would be taken to the Head, and each give their side of the story and (pause) it's the same old question. What do you say (silence)?

Remembering that at least one entire class of children had witnessed the incident I asked if the children in her school were the sort who would want to tell their teacher if they saw something like this happening. Helen said:

> Yes, they would want to tell ... I think that by and large they are good children.

In our final meeting we returned to this account, and I finally explained that it had actually happened outside her own classroom door. Helen seemed reluctant to discuss the incident further or to make any direct comment on it, but said:

> You feel so helpless though ... the cleaner at our school, the top one, she said something about 'Oh Pakis, I can't be doing with them'. I didn't know what to say (pause). The cleaner in my classroom said 'Oh isn't she terrible, Helen?' in a jokey sort of way, but it's such a contentious issue and if I said 'I'm sorry I don't agree with that' (pause). I'm ashamed that I didn't.

In an interview with the Head, I also presented the incident as a fictional scenario and asked whether it could happen in her school. She replied that there were reports of gang-centred racial attacks in the area. When I asked what she would do if a similar situation developed in her school, she said she would 'just have to look at it from a totally different point of view', adding:

> I mean I touch wood when I say this but at the moment that isn't an issue at the school. There has been within the last three months an issue developing outside the school, not with *our* children, with the *older* children, with teenagers ... there have been quite a lot of disturbances at nights. That I think might well (pause) I think in twelve months, two years time, that it could well work its way down.

The Head stated that the staff were all well aware of these incidents. Yet even though the staff had been informed of the 'disturbances', there was no indication that the issue needed to be discussed with the children. This elegantly echoes Helen's first school experience, as both institutions were cognisant of localised racial incidents but neither felt it appropriate to confront the issue as a staff or to broach the subject with their children. It is interesting also to relate this reluctance to acknowledge racial violence in predominantly white areas to HM Inspectorate of Constabulary's identification of an escalation of incidents in these areas. Racial attacks reported in Cheshire, for example, rose from nil in 1989 to 98 in 1993/4. When I asked Helen outright if she had any personal experience of racial tension in the school, she replied:

> I have never heard anything said or got any vibes off the children. Whether that's different in Year Five and Year Six I don't know. I did notice the other morning when I was walking to school on the wall it was spray painted 'Pakis out'.

In between the racial incident and the end of the course, Helen went along on a visit to a Mosque and then a Sikh temple (more detailed reference to the latter is made in Rachel's story). The visit to the Mosque was not received particularly well by some of the students. One told me:

> To a certain extent there is an English way of doing things and I think it should be protected. A good example of that was all that about women not being allowed into the Mosque if they are menstruating. It's all bollocks.

The visit to the Gurdwara, on the other hand, elicited some praise, particularly as one of the senior members had explained to the students how his daughter had been the focus for several discussions on race and religion in her school, and gave examples of the positive outcomes that had been reached in conjunction with a sensitive class teacher. Helen was impressed by this experience and had questioned the speaker at length about how his daughter coped with this kind of attention. In our last interview it was clear that the experience had made her think:

Russell	So what has changed you?
Helen	I think perhaps having confidence as a teacher and seeing your role as a teacher (pause) not like a demigod but you do have certain responsibilities and I think it is very important to stand up for what you believe. At times.
Russell	So that is part of your growing professional confidence?
Helen	Yes, probably.
Russell	With the race issue and the question I just asked, did it come into your mind about the story I told you?
Helen	Yes, yes.
Russell	There wasn't a policy or...?
Helen	I mean I felt that was lacking last time and I said to you that in the classes I had been in there were some Asian children. There was one girl, Chani in Year Three and I felt very much that she was in isolation, but I still feel that by bringing it to the fore you can put focus on the child and it can easily lead to them feeling even more isolated.
Russell	That is the opposite of what Mr Devgon said at the temple last week about his daughter and how her teacher used her to raise a lot of these issues in the class.

Helen	Didn't I ask him this question?
Russell	I think you did.
Helen	I was wondering about how it felt from their point of view to have the focus put on them. I think it depends on the children. Like Chani, I tried to talk to Chani about a topic on food and she drew a plate of sausage and chips and I said 'I am sure you don't eat that, Chani', this lesson was about their favourite meal and I said 'Is that what you eat?' and then it came out slowly that she ate rice and different things like that and she didn't eat meat.
Russell	Was she feeling under pressure to...?
Helen	She wanted to be the same (pause) but it would crush her confidence to have to stand up and talk about her differences.

However this exchange is read, it brings a number of issues to the fore. Helen says that she feels 'it is very important to stand up for what you believe', yet qualifies it with 'at times', thereby making the distinction that there are also times when this might not be appropriate. What then follows is an example of how she negotiates this in her classroom. Having heard a Sikh father praise his daughter's predominantly white primary school for having the courage to take on board issues of ethnicity in the classroom, and expressing admiration for all concerned, Helen remains reluctant to begin the same process. In the food lesson, Helen interprets Chani's drawing of sausages as 'wanting to be the same'. But this drawing could equally be interpreted as 'not feeling comfortable to articulate the ways in which she is different'.

In appealing to the notion of protecting the child from having to acknowledge her own ethnic status, Helen overlooks the impossibility of the child disguising it. Everything about her physical appearance, dress, language and culture defined her as different to her white colleagues. Although Chani should certainly not have been immediately coerced into talking about her beliefs, this lesson presented a perfect opportunity to bring some of these wider issues to bear. Why did Helen accept that so doing had been valuable for the Sikh leader's daughter but not recognise or accept similar opportunities in her own classroom? It is possible that Helen made a distinction between her classroom and a Gurdwara as suitable places to discuss issues of ethnicity, or that she genuinely felt threatened by the idea of raising the issue and potentially causing distress to Chani? Possibly the school's ethos was not hospitable to such avenues of discussion and it would have seemed contrived and somehow inappropriate. Whatever the reasons, Helen reached the end of her course, was about to qualify as a primary teacher, was working in the most ethnically mixed classroom I witnessed, was aware (by this time) of racial tension and violence in the school, and *still* felt unable to acknowledge ethnic identity openly in her classroom in a wider educational context.

Helen's story is exceptional in that I accidentally witnessed a significant incident that became the focal point for my questioning and opened up a new dialogue between all concerned. For the vast majority of my sample, however, issues of race and ethnicity were simply not part of the dialogue that constituted any part of their teacher education. Helen's case is exceptional also because she had been placed in a relatively ethnically diverse school and so had clear opportunities to address the issue, whereas for others this simply was not the case. Interestingly, while recognising that these elements were present within her initial teacher education, Helen did not seem to engage with the issue beyond what appeared to be a casual rejection of racist terminology. Her interviews show that she considers herself to be 'sensitive to the issues' and 'converted', but that the input from her course did little or nothing to challenge or develop this state. The need to bring beginning teachers to a point where they recognise and challenge the social and cultural biases they bring with them to the course has been well documented (Eggleston 1993, Gaine, 1995), and there are particular resonances for those trained in the 'white highlands' who go on to teach in inner city areas:

> Students must be taught the importance of sharing the child's community, as too many inner-city teachers come in from outside and never really perceive the needs of the community group, they impose their own values and education...White students need to understand the 'black experience', and this should not be interpreted or taught as a cultural or ethnic experience; they need to understand the realities of the

day-to-day lives of black people living within the confines of white social
practices, norms and structures (Siraj-Blatchford, 1993a p32).

For students in my sample who intended to remain within the
'white highlands' in which they qualified (my impression was that
this would be the vast majority and this impression was to be supported by the 1993 inspection of primary school training
(OFSTED, 1993 pp2-4)), it appears that this level of realisation is
not going to be part of their professional development as newly
qualified teachers. The subject of multicultural or antiracist education is in danger of becoming a non-issue, or one that exists in
word only. I can find no evidence from my data to claim that any
aspect of Helen's initial teacher education brought about any professional challenge of individual prejudice or bias, or any greater
sense of critical questioning. At the end of her course, Helen's
views on the need for multicultural issues to be addressed remain
at the same level as the staff's in her first school in the first month
of her course, meaning (for her) that addressing the issue would
raise problems that were not there in the first place. Despite the
sensitive account passed on by the representative of the temple that
detailed how beneficial discussion had been for everyone concerned at the school, Helen remained convinced that it would only
serve to further isolate any ethnic minority children she might
teach.

So Helen apparently reflected and ultimately legitimised the
school's lethargy, incorporating it in her own practice. The school
clearly did nothing to address a grave and violent issue which appeared to be escalating. The Head acknowledged that racially
motivated fights took place outside the school building in the even-
ings; there were members of the staff who held questionable views
on race and who were prepared to use racist insults inside the
school; and the children were adding to this tension by demonstrating racist aggression openly in the school, yet the issue was
still not one to be discussed. Helen herself walked past graffiti
reading 'Pakis Out' on her way into school; she was aware of the
violence and the name-calling; she allowed the cleaners to use
racist language in her own classroom unchecked, saying afterwards 'What do you say?' and 'You feel so helpless'. Remember

that Helen still saw herself as 'sensitive to the issues' and that she perceived multicultural education input from the university as merely 'preaching to the converted'. It would appear that to Helen, racism remains a fact of life that is to be morally condemned but ultimately tolerated because she can do little or nothing about it in her professional capacity.

'I don't have a problem'

Helen's insistence that she was somehow enlightened about equality issues was not uncommon; students tended to see this as an area that they had no need to address. Right from the start of their courses, when they were questioned they revealed an under-standing that relied heavily on vague notions of perceiving the children as individuals and treating everyone the same. During my initial round of interviews, typical responses were:

> As far as I am concerned they are all children, they're not girls and boys ... a child is a child, it doesn't matter what sex they are or what colour they are, what religion (Beginning teacher on university-based course).

> I think it is better to have relationships with the children in your class because they are individuals, they are not Tommy who's black, Billy who's in a wheelchair, they are Tommy and Billy and the wheelchair and the colour bit doesn't even come close. It's more about what is going on here (indicates her heart) that I am interested in, and I get very cross with people who start treating them in different ways because of that, whether they mean to or not. It makes me very angry (Beginning teacher on university-based course).

> They are individuals. I don't look at them as brown or white, or boys and girls, it's how they are as a class. Their personalities (Beginning teacher on school-based course).

These statements highlight just how complicated this apparently simplistic notion of individuality can be. The students were un-animous in their concern that they 'treat all children the same', but their conceptions of what this meant in practice, or how this impacts on the children in front of them, were vague and ill-defined. The second respondent, for example, claims that the crucial aspect of the issue for her is the teacher's relationship with the child, but then describes how her (hypothetical) relationship with Tommy would be based on systematic disregard for his ethnic identity. The quality of any relationship where one participant is perceived as white by proxy must surely be dubious, but when that relationship is between teacher and learner, the underlying assumptions are worrying. Similarly, in consecutive sentences the third respondent illustrates the oversimplification of this approach: she begins by stating that her intention is to conceptualise the children in her care as individuals, yet then asserts that she does not want to recognise their colour or their sex. Her argument then revolves as she suppresses individuality by trying to see children as 'a class', and revolves yet again when she ends her argument with another reminder about the value of their individual personalities.

The naive desire to treat children as individuals is equated un-problematically with 'treating them all the same'. This in turn equates with the notion that it is somehow admirable or desirable that the teacher should ignore the fact that Tommy is black even though the reality that every child and adult can see that he is black, or that the teacher should ignore Billy's wheelchair despite the reality that every child in the classroom can see that he cannot move around without it. It would seem as though the concept of 'child' here becomes the exact opposite of 'individual' and instead becomes a category. While they want to maintain the sense of the child as individual, these students show their willingness to cate-gorise them in an homogeneous group labelled 'child', where even skin colour or disability can be conceptually disregarded in the 'proxifying' process. Again, we have seen this before:

> Disability as an equal opportunities issue was raised on a few occasions during my fieldwork, as was the sense that racism was a problem of the past, confirming the view that beginning teachers perceive equal oppor-tunities as an unproblematic issue (Haydn, 1997 p100).

The issue of disability arose occasionally throughout my time in schools, even though it had not been part of my research design. One lecturer commented on these issues in more detail:

> We do some discussion groups in the first year and one of them is looking at bias and insensitivity in maths materials ... what is alarming in some ways is the almost dismissive way that some students can look at some things like that and say 'Oh it's alright now, it's a lot better than it was', and see it as a problem solved ... They recognised that disability was

the issue of the nineties, and that in some ways things have moved. What was a bit disappointing in a way was that the fact that they saw one problem as having been and gone and another one, the issue of disability, had replaced it rather than seeing it as something which is ever present but appearing in different ways.

So this maths lecturer was able to identify a trend in the thinking of his beginning teachers that the issue of racism had been solved (sic) and at least the issue of bias and stereotypes in support materials had been raised as part of the course outline. However, this was not part of the taught experience of my sample group. Clearly there are elements of a four year course that are going to be lost on a one year PGCE, and equal opportunities issues seem to be one casualty. Although this maths lecturer could articulate numerous examples of materials and ideas he had used to raise equality issues with his students, he could no longer achieve this on any of his current modules due to the time constraints placed on his courses and the drive to cover more tangible subject matter from the National Curriculum.

No time for social justice

This confirms recent teacher educator discourse analysis which claims that there is a discrepancy between the desire to debate wider social and pedagogical issues with beginning teachers and the theoretical structures and discourses of lectures in which 'social transformation is explicitly rejected (and) social pessimism is firmly embedded' (Grundy and Hatton, 1995 p22). The teacher educators in my study asserted repeatedly that there was simply insufficient time to cover wider issues such as multicultural education and equal opportunities but, equally, they were convinced that someone else covered it – usually, lecturers under the RE provision made by the university. However, as one lecturer pointed out: '...you can do RE in a non-multicultural way I think, but I don't know if it is done in a non-multicultural way or not'. Typical responses from lecturers at universities were:

We haven't even talked about it and I think that is a pity that we don't, I suppose I just hope that my colleagues portray the same kind of feel about teaching. But that's an assumption isn't it?

I don't think I do it as well as I could ... I know I don't do it well enough and you know (pause) I'm desperate to do it better.

They (the beginning teachers) may pick it up by osmosis, it may be there and they may never be able to sort of spell it out and say 'This is actually important'. I don't know. Perhaps I ought to ask them at the end of the course.

I think there is quite a lot of it going on ... it is just good practice and it might not appear in written format. I think the danger is that if you do put it on your course outline and say 'We will be dealing with it in session five' and it actually becomes itemised, then there is a danger that it is the only place it gets dealt with rather than it being a natural part...

Adam	(*Lecturer on university-based course*) The ideal thing would be that it permeates the curriculum area, but the issue should be something that (pause) you know (pause) it should be focused on specifically as an explicit element within the course...
Russell	You said that there are other areas of the curriculum where you know that multicultural education is a feature...
Adam	I don't know how much (pause) in all honesty I don't know how much it is emphasised...
Russell	Is there any time when everyone gets together and talks about things like multicultural education?
Jane	(*Lecturer on school-based course*) No.

One lecturer who claimed to teach a directly multicultural element in her course explained how she saw it as an integral part of the process of understanding the musical elements of the National Curriculum. She told me:

It's hard. The only way I can bring it to the students is through video, I bring videos and obviously recorded music so that they can actually see it, but you know... it's very much reliant on people's whims and fancies isn't it? Nobody knows that I'm making the point, apart from the students. Nobody on the staff here knows what I do (Lecturer on university-based course).

Although this lecturer could show how multicultural education was a cross-curricular feature in her teaching, when I pressed her she admitted that this was only true of a part of her four year BA(Ed) course. So this was another case where multicultural education had been effectively erased from a PGCE course.

Thus the teacher educators felt that issues such as multicultural education and racial equality were often lost in the drive to respond to the demands of the National Curriculum, and hoped that somehow these issues would permeate through enhancing students' understanding of what constituted 'good practice'. Although the sense of tutor 'helplessness' was a recurrent theme, Grundy and Hatton's report suggests otherwise, concluding that many discourses with students actually provide opportunities and openings for considerations of equality and fairness:

> While the recognition of multiple non-transformative ideological discourses might appear to make the situation more complex and less amenable to intervention, this is not necessarily so. Analysis of these discourses has revealed spaces and silences which provide possibilities of challenging and transcending the limits of the discourse (Grundy and Hatton, 1995 p22).

While the cry of insufficient time or opportunity was repeated across the entire range of subjects, there were some lecturers who claimed still to be finding spaces to incorporate equality issues within at least one of their subject lectures, but further questions narrowed this again to only the four year course. Only one lecturer could say that she managed it with her PGCE group. She was responsible for some of the English work, and proudly showed me the children's texts she had used to demonstrate bias and prejudice in literature for the young. Most other tutors could point me towards effective support materials they had used in the past and recount tales about how well these sessions had gone, but when pushed they would invariably admit that they were talking about lessons from some years earlier and that this aspect of their teaching was no longer a focus on their courses.

Moreover, the lecturers who raised these issues and produced support materials were based in the institution in which this study took place, and I assume that they had some idea about my research. None of the lecturers at the institution where my work was less familiar produced such evidence. Sometimes lecturers would tell me about optional study elements on their courses where equal opportunities was included as a potential choice, but again, when pushed, it turned out that it was rarely chosen by a student. Lecturers and tutors at both institutions typically imagined that the issue of multicultural education permeated the entire course but again when I asked for examples of how this worked within a lecturer's own practice I heard the same story about the lack of time, the need to ensure National Curriculum content was covered in detail and an assurance that they were sure it happened somewhere on other parts of the course.

Some teacher educators who described their past involvement with multicultural education now felt frustrated at their lack of opportunity to incorporate it in their teaching, and felt they were alone in considering it worthy of attention. These lecturers invariably said that their commitment to equality issues was personal rather than the result of any formal training, discussion or requirement by the institution:

Russell	So all the things that you have learnt about race are to do with you as a professional rather than say staff development here or...
Linda	(*Lecturer on university-based course*) Oh God yes (laughs).
Russell	It's all to do with your experiences as a teacher?
Linda	(laughs) It's *nothing* to do with what I've experienced here. Sadly. Nothing.
Russell	How do you think this (multicultural education) is co-ordinated across the faculty?
Susan	(*Lecturer on university-based course*) It isn't (pause) there is nothing written down, there is nothing co-ordinated and if it comes anywhere in the course as a discreet unit it would come in EPS but there is no policy.
Russell	Is anybody responsible for multicultural education as an issue?
Adam	No, I'm not aware of anybody actually co-ordinating.

When questioned about multicultural issues students often said that they would want to challenge racist behaviour in their class-rooms. In view of the university's inability to tackle these issues it is unsurprising that they then revealed a poor grasp of their own attitudes. These findings concur with Gollnick's claim that:

> Research is needed on how to prepare whites, who make up 90 per cent of the teacher candidates in colleges and universities, to work effectively in communities that are culturally different than their own. Can we teach candidates to recognize and overcome their own biases? (Gollnick, 1992 p238).

While teaching students to 'recognize and overcome their own biases' is problematic, if not philosophically impossible, beginning teachers certainly need to work on identifying how their own pre-judices operate and realise that their biases might not be appro-priate in classrooms with children from cultures significantly dif-ferent from their own. Whereas this is an issue for teacher educators in general, I suggest that it is more pressing and even more difficult in the 'white highlands', where beginning teachers are even less likely to have teaching and learning experiences that will allow them to confront their own prejudices and biases. Multi-cultural teacher training in areas where there are no schools with multi-ethnic populations is clearly problematic. I was made aware of this difficulty several times during my data collection:

Russell	Did you have any ethnic minority children in your class?
Grace	No.
Russell	None at all?
Grace	I'm not sure of their origins but I think one girl (pause) she was a dark girl (pause) neither of them were black but she had white parents (pause) I'm not sure about the other little boy. He was dark. There was a handful in the whole school...
Russell	Did you say you are going to (school name) next?
Grace	Hmmm (pause) it's another nice school.
Russell	Do you think you will find many ethnic minority children there?
Grace	No. I know I've been spoilt. I know that.

While this student indicates a misunderstanding about the ethnicity of the children she had worked with, even more dangerous is her equation of 'nice' schools and being 'spoilt' by being placed in predominantly white schools. This inability in students to recognise their own ignorance raised itself in several ways. Another first interview drew the following exchange:

Russell   Have you got any ethnic minority children in your school?

Lauren   No, I haven't seen any at all (pause) but I'm from an ethnic (pause) I'm from Wolverhampton, so that's really, you know, multicultural.

Russell   So are there things from your own background then that you would bring to your teaching? Things that you might know about other cultures?

Lauren   (pause) I don't think so.

Responses of this kind to the subject of multicultural education suggest more than an idealised naiveté in these beginning teachers. A pattern emerges. Each student is able to articulate a variety of reasons why the issues of race might be important on a perceived national scale but are not specifically relevant to them. Typically, these denials were qualified with the suggestion that they could see how other 'less enlightened' students might require formal instruction in the subject. Lauren, for example, readily admits that she knows nothing about children from other cultures but equally as readily argues that multicultural education was not really an issue for her course to address.

Joining the club

I began to think that the lack of opportunity to explore equality was due not only to their conspicuous absence at the university but also to the professional relationships students established during their school experiences. For example, Helen's Headteacher told me that:

I don't think that staff should stay at a school for a long time, I think that five or six years and they ought to be moving on, otherwise you become very inflexible and you see one way of doing it and there are other ways of doing it.

This was despite the fact that she had been in place over twenty years, and the Deputy/teacher-mentor had been in the same school for 32 years. These points are not incidental to Helen's education: When I asked about her progress, the mentor said:

> What I've been pleased to see is that Helen has stayed behind for all our staff meetings and she has taken part on all our INSET ... she has developed a great sense of loyalty, and that's lovely.

This lovely sense of loyalty, the repeated description of the school as 'happy' and Helen's wish that she could get a job there all began to suggest a situation which was far too cosy. This may help to explain why potentially contentious issues were not discussed and why, even in the face of racial abuse and violence, the Head, her staff and the student all sought to maintain Chris Gaine's facade of 'no problem here' (Gaine, 1995). Helen confirmed this interpretation:

Russell	How would you describe your relationship with (mentor's name)?
Helen	Very very good. She's a nice, homely, normal person. They're the best people. I can't do with ... (silence)
Russell	She was sensitive to your needs?
Helen	That's right, yes. Sort of a motherly figure...

There are important issues that rise out of Helen's perception of her mentor and the way this perception was reciprocated and reinforced. Primary schools are known for particularly close relationships, both on a professional and personal basis. One study of student roles and personal relationships during primary school teaching practices recognised that 'personality characteristics can become highly significant' (Hodgkinson, 1992 p2). Students are naturally keen to 'fit in' with the ethos of the school, and they know that among the criteria upon which they are judged is their ability to forge strong, productive relationships in the school. Similarly, all my professional experience tells me that having accepted the responsibility of guiding a beginning teacher, mentors and supervising teachers are willing to do whatever they can to 'get them through the practice'. Many will invite students to their own homes, lend their own resources and so on. It is reasonable to suppose that closer personal bonds lead to closer professional understanding although this was not necessarily the case with Helen and her mentor.

More recent research into mentor-student relationships within school-based primary ITE suggests that senior managers often do not perceive the process as being beneficial to the school, meaning that although mentors may have much to offer, they often operate without proper support from the school (Edwards, 1996a pp58-60). Similarly, it has been suggested that schools have not yet demonstrated a desire to change their practice in order to accommodate their new role. Quite the reverse seems to be true, as schools see successful students as those who are able to replicate existing practice unproblematically:

> The actual practices of mentors in classrooms suggest that mentoring is an essentially conservative activity with the maintenance of the status quo as a priority. Not rocking the boat was a prevailing metaphor (Edwards, 1997 p28).

What then when beginning teachers with simplistic notions about pedagogical processes come to rely on replicating the practice of their mentors without fully understanding what might be taking place? These 'empty procedural tricks' (Furlong and Maynard, 1995 p156) might be interpreted as success in the classroom if the mentor is not able or prepared to develop a more critical understanding about the nature of teaching and learning. This would appear to have been closer to the reality of the relationship between Helen and her mentor than any critical training model, and responses from both during interview supported the notion that there was little to be gained from this practice beyond some friendly support for a fellow professional.

In our first interview after the placement, Helen reported that she already felt 'like a member of staff'. She claimed that:

> I am not the sort of person who can operate at their best if they feel they are working under a cloud or if that relationship isn't there ... I really do feel for other people who haven't got that.

It is surely significant that Helen referred to her mentor on several occasions (both formally and informally) in 'motherly' terms, describing her as 'homely', 'lovely', 'nice', and 'normal'. She acknowledged her mentor as the most influential person in her training, and reinforced the image of the supportive parent when she stressed that 'she gave me enough rope, she didn't mollycoddle me'. This relationship would appear to have been reciprocated if not established by the mentor, who saw her role primarily as helping Helen gain confidence in the classroom. Her idea of success was epitomised when, with less than three months of the course remaining, she could say: 'Helen, I've got to go with our maths co-ordinator and some other members of staff to work out a problem that we are having. Do you mind, tomorrow if I am in and out of the classroom?'

One mentor in a different school acknowledged that such situations could easily arise: 'You have to be on your guard sometimes when they (the students) say 'Why don't I just stay here?'. You know it has got a bit too cosy then'. Reflecting that she had been teaching in the same school for thirty two years, Helen's mentor told me:

> One of the things she (Helen) said last week to me, she said 'I wish ... ' she was looking at the circular, she said 'I wish there was a job, I wish there was a job here'. She said, 'I've been so happy', and I said, 'Yes, but you haven't been to many other places yet' and she said, 'I can understand you staying. I can understand all these years because you've been happy haven't you?' and I think that is very important. Something which she did say, which surprised me, because I said 'Oh don't say that', and she said 'I don't think (pause) I don't think I want to make a success of my career, I'm not career minded, promotion-wise'.

Though it is understandable that a teacher might want to stay at the 'chalk face' of the classroom there are dangers that beginning teachers might perceive this as the model to mirror at the start of their careers. The statement above is evidence of how primary school-based courses founded on overly comfortable, non-critical relationships can easily fall into a parochial or provincial mentality at this crucial point in the student's professional development. This ultimately inhibits the growth of a young, dynamic and creative teaching force.

Equally significant, when I asked if she would have liked experience of another school, Helen said that despite having spent almost her entire year in the same primary school, she did not. When I asked about the future, she replied: 'I just want to get a nice school and (pause) somewhere that is supportive. I don't necessarily want easy children, I just want a supportive staff'. Her mentor told me that Helen had been to look around two schools that had advertised vacancies, but had said she was wary of working in a school that differed significantly from the one in which she was trained, particularly with regards to methods of assessment. This may well be another issue to be taken on board by the designers of school-based courses. If students like Helen are encouraged to develop a 'great sense of loyalty' to one school (and a parallel sense of loyalty to one system of teaching and learning), their reluctance to break away from that model when seeking employment is understandable.

There are particular resonances with this sense of loyalty and the issue of multicultural education. Helen's thinking around the subject apparently remained static and unchallenged by her course, but even more dangerous is the supposition that it will remain so. Once qualified, she actively sought employment in an institution that was unlikely to challenge her thinking. Helen's acceptance of the status quo, her desire to work in a homely, supportive atmosphere and her demonstrated intention to leave contentious issues untouched, combine to suggest that this newly qualified professional will not want to begin challenging her own prejudices and biases and develop a model of professional practice that is based on a real sense of critical reflection.

There are several other significant issues related to Helen and school-based ITE for intending primary teachers that arise out of my data. Helen openly praised the university for placing her in a supportive school that remedied an earlier problem with her placement (which was in no way related to her practice). The course leader informed me that Helen's school and mentor had both been specifically identified as a potential safety net for any student who might have a problematic placement. The school was one in which the university could 'guarantee good practice', the mentor was known for her sensitivity towards the needs of the student and her implicit understanding of the pace of learning for beginning teachers. So Helen's placement was at a school seen as a bedrock, and which could be counted on in times of need to exemplify the dynamics of the course and to ensure that a student who had had difficulties (for whatever reason) would now have the best possible chance of passing.

Training inadequancies in partnership schools

There are unresolved training issues also. Although the school had been selected because the university valued its good practice and because the staff had worked well with teaching practice students on university-based programmes in the past, the Head told me:

> We went into this without any training and I just feel that I'm not totally sure what we should be doing. I just feel that if it is going to go over to that model then we do need more guidance as to exactly what our role is. My other big worry is the load on staff.

This is a dangerous admission and one which the university would no doubt prefer to deny, pointing to course documentation they sent out to schools as supporting evidence of their involvement (I return to this issue later in Laura's story). Helen's mentor gave me a different story, relating how she had attended an evening meeting at the university where someone (sic): 'just said what he was hoping to do and how our part would be very, very important'. She was unable to offer any other evidence of her preparation as a mentor. She explained that there had been a follow-up meeting in school led by the course leader, but said that she had not attended. When I asked if she had received any formal training, she replied: 'No. I don't know if there is any or not'.

Weaknesses in the process of selecting schools and then preparing them to be institutions of ITE were identified in the HMI Report which preceded the shift towards greater emphasis on school-based teacher education.

> The generality of class teachers receive virtually no training or induction for their role in teacher training and as a result may be uncertain and confused about what is expected of them (DES, 1991 p34 point 73).

This Report concludes that: 'There is little point in seeking to improve training by making it more school-based if students do not learn from the most experienced and successful teachers' (DES, 1991 p34, point 73). Obviously this is now somewhat dated, and closer partnerships between ITE faculties and school-based mentors are being established, but my data still suggests that the situation has by no means been resolved (as I discuss further in Laura's story). The HMI's suggestion that the training of mentors for the school-based programme has been in some ways deficient would seem to be precisely exemplified in Helen's 'hand picked' school, where the Head stated that no training at all had been given, and the mentor did not know whether such training even existed.

Other misunderstandings were evident when talking about provision for PGCE students. For example, Helen's Head stated that: 'We take the view that we are expected to more or less throw them in at the deep end'. This conception of teacher education was not uncommon (see Laura's story for example). Helen's time in the school was scheduled to last from November until June so there was surely time enough for the school to devise an induction programme that would be more than 'throwing them in at the deep end', even though the school 'went into this without any training'.

Social justice at the chalk face
So Helen's story reveals several issues that need resolution, each related to the views expressed by school staff concerning their notions of themselves as teacher educators, the negotiated role that beginning primary teachers adopt over long periods in the school, and the obvious discrepancy between the rhetoric and the reality of mentor training. If it were hoped that multicultural education and issues of social justice would become part of an ongoing training dialogue between beginning teachers and their mentors, it would seem that those hopes were misguided.

It seems to be taken for granted by all concerned that by working within the particular environment of the primary classroom, the beginning teacher will be exposed to general and wide-ranging issues related to teaching and learning. One examination of planning and evaluative conversations between mentors and beginning teachers suggested that: 'Mentors' own emphasis on language in the concept formation of children is not evident in the way they instructed the student-teachers' and that mentors found it difficult to move from 'procedural to propositional knowledge' (Edwards and Collison, 1995 p275). They report that mentors were generous in their desire to create 'safe contexts in which students could acquire a repertoire of useful behaviours and engage in trial and error learning' (Edwards and Collison, 1995 p275). This resonates with Helen's experiences in school. The 'safe' context in which to work was an obvious and overt concern of her mentor, but the emphasis on 'a repertoire of useful behaviours' and the dearth of instructional dialogue which went beyond particular needs in the classroom meant that Helen was practically and conceptually locked into the models and dynamics of her institution, so her concerns about employment in a different context might have been justified.

The HMI Report (DES, 1991) raised several other relevant concerns. In its commentary it made particular reference to the role of primary schools in the shift towards school-based ITE, and the difficulties in achieving sufficient quality of provision within the PGCE course. Concern was expressed about how mentors were chosen (typically by Heads who understandably may prefer not to tie up their strongest, most experienced teachers for almost a year), which could mean that students did not always receive the best experience of training a school could offer.

> The organisation of primary schools and the small size of them, together with the heavy teaching loads undertaken by most primary teachers, mean that they do not generally have the capacity or the range of expertise needed to take on significant additional training responsibilities without considerable support (DES, 1991 p4 point 5 vii).

Another study of training in primary schools claimed that almost a third of students felt that 'their teachers had insufficient time for supervising students' (Hodgkinson, 1992 p3). It is interesting to bear this in mind when looking at mentoring schemes for secondary schools, where it has been suggested that 'Support, assessment and development requires additional time input and at its extreme may involve up to three additional hours per day' (Glover et al., 1994 p26). Since students in primary schools have the whole curriculum to deal with rather than a single subject (although this could change with the advent of KS2/3 courses and the emphasis on subject specialism in primary schools) and since 'free periods' are largely unknown, curriculum provision is even more likely to override 'lesser issues' such as multicultural education. It is increasingly acknowledged that the nature of primary education clashes with National Curriculum directives as there are not enough subject specialists in the typical primary school to cover each area with real skill and understanding, and many teachers have to take on more than one subject.

Some of these issues are explored in another study which looked into the changes in teacher confidence and competence levels in small rural primary schools in response to the demands of the National Curriculum. This report described how such schools had established cluster groups to pool human resources and had begun to use local advisor assistance to greater effect, with the result that the schools were in significant professional flux, and this change had, in some instances, meant that 'for the first time issues of pedagogy as opposed to planning and assessment were beginning to be addressed' (Hargreaves *et al,* 1996 p98). If Hargreaves' study is indicative of the ways small rural primary schools are having to reinvent their educational processes to comply with current legislation, it seems unlikely that the preparation of school-based beginning teachers will be centre stage. On the contrary, beginning teachers placed in institutions such as these will probably experience a frustrating and contradictory year of learning.

Siraj-Blatchford identified a political climate which 'made it increasingly difficult to promote equality issues which are not only deemed marginal; efforts have actually been made by some on the right to take them completely off the agenda' (1993b p90). It is not too difficult to interpret the dogged adherence to school-based ITE as one example of how to make this happen. As I argue later, there are clear indications that more recent legislation on education was provoked because initial teacher education was seen as in some way deficient and needed to be overhauled. It is strange therefore that there is so little documented evidence of these deficiencies. Similarly, there seems to be an equally unspoken presumption that school-based ITE is the solution and again, little documented evidence of this being so. The conclusion that the shift into school-based ITE is to serve political ends is difficult to resist. It certainly fits in with the Teacher Training Agency's (TTA) proposals for the immediate future (Tysome, 1996a and b). Objections to the common university practice of 'top-slicing' budgets have helped support the claim that school-based training is potentially cheaper than the traditional university-based B.Ed or PGCE, although recent evidence suggests the contrary (Whiting *et al.*, 1996 p71). Secondly, it effectively removes from power teacher educators who have been variously described as trendy leftie, ideologically moti-vated, and as irrelevant to the real business of teaching. Finally it brings into being a new, technicist teaching force whose training may use the rhetoric of 'reflective practice' but in effect teaches students to mirror 'successful practice', not to question, not to be critical of their own practice or of wider philosophical practice and to conceive of and respond to the developing needs of their own school in the arena of a competitive market place. At the end of her course, and during our final interview, Helen looked back over her equal opportunities input and observed:

> We just seemed to be talking about things that we knew already, we didn't seem to be really going anywhere, just confirming things we were already aware of.

Helen echoes her mentor's insistence that the school was a 'happy' one, but Helen said this *after* she had been told about the racial incident. To Helen it was still possible to describe a school as 'happy' even when she knew that racial harassment took place in the corridor outside her classroom. She still maintained that the school was 'happy' even when admitting that there were behavioural problems that she had had to deal with while 'quaking in (my) bloody boots'. There seemed to be nothing in Helen's training which had encouraged a genuinely reflective practitioner. Even the reality of racial attacks outside her classroom and 'Pakis Out' scrawled on the wall outside the school seemed unable to loosen her adherence to a cosy model of teaching as an uncom-plicated and unchallenging profession. I had to conclude that some of the inadequate practice my research had revealed had now become part of Helen's own teaching and this sat rather uncomfortably with my original impression of the teaching and learning I had witnessed in Helen's classroom.

It is important to locate these concerns historically, just as a study of 211 teacher education courses suggests that there are 'significant weaknesses in the current partnership models of teacher education' and that scope for training schools to move towards the model of teacher training proposed by the TTA are 'decidedly limited' (Gardiner, 1996a p5). Moreover, the study casts serious doubt on the perception that HEIs were attempting to create 'child centred' or progressive teachers. The way that school centred ITE has become dominant does not convince one that children are at the heart of the exercise. One teacher educator described the current situation as:

> ...a situation in which school-based courses are badly overstretching an already beleaguered teaching profession; are forcing too many students in training to focus on survival rather than developing a range of skills as young teachers; and are selling the nation's children badly short (Lowe, 1995 p91).

Lowe provides a powerful reminder that the entire debate is about the life chances of young children, and the suggestion that they are being 'sold short' by their education is one that resonates loudly through the ensuing stories.

Teacher educators need to be aware that training experiences such as Helen's offer insights into the way we see the development of our teaching and learning communities. Teacher training is about providing inexperienced people with the facilities to recognise their *potential* in schools and establish the baseline for ongoing professional development over a significant period of time. Helen's story suggests that a different conception of teacher training is in the ascendant – one where it is important that the student demonstrates an ability to achieve professional competence in a short space of time and to conform unproblematically to existing practice – even when that practice is acknowledged as unsatisfactory, impoverished and negligent. It is the school mentor's duty to establish criteria whereby the student can be seen to replicate existing attitudes, behaviours and teaching styles – even when these merely confirm the inadequacies of poor practice. The children in this model are not afforded a voice. It is only by conceiving of children as powerless receptacles within this process that the model can work.

When racism occurs within this pedagogical framework it is easy to see how it is conceived and handled by those in authority. They disregarded it completely. When teacher training concerns itself primarily with demonstrably achieved targets and mechanical processes, it denies the diversity of children's experience and undermines the complicated business of teaching and learning. Consequently, when students meet the reality of racist attacks, they have no strategies to deal with them, no understanding of how racism works, nor any real concept of how it affects children's lives. The system that trains them does not allow much deviation: it is there to measure performance, and it is much easier for all concerned to simply deny that issues such as racism exist.

For racism to be dealt with effectively within a teacher training model which is becoming increasingly school-based, it is essential that mentors become active in the process of challenging students' preconceptions and biases. This is not easy when many mentors have yet to achieve this condition for themselves. Consequently, the only way forward is to ensure that training criteria related to race and multicultural issues appear as part of the qualification process. Universities need to work with schools to ensure that mentors fully understand the need for this to happen at school level, and (most problematically) why it is particularly important in predominantly white schools. More fundamentally, students need to conceive of children not as passive vessels waiting for wisdom, but as part of a teaching and learning relationship which is too easily forgotten in the technicist model of training. The following story begins to illustrate what happens when students are not encouraged to acknowledge and develop and assess this relationship.

Chapter 4

Kim's Story

Multicultural education: whose job is it anyway?

I first met Kim at one of the small group meetings with another new intake of beginning teachers. I recorded in the field notes of these meetings that she made no particular impression on me and that she spoke out only once, to tell me that she had wanted to enter the profession after she had helped out in her local school prior to coming on the course. She was enrolled on the university-based course and as only ten of the year's intake agreed to be involved with my research I had no choice in my sample. After our first formal interview however, I was more than keen to include her as one of my detailed life studies for the coming year.

This was partly because I had recognised that once settled into the course, Kim was confident, articulate and likely to tell me precisely what she thought about her training. Reviewing my field notes however, I realise her responses to my early questions had interested me – firstly in her openly expressed philosophy of education. She came from a family of teachers, had connections with the local brownies and guides and was confident about her reasons for wanting to teach:

> It's just sort of been natural. If you look at my CV, all the jobs I've done, all the experiences I've had, it just points in one direction basically (laughs). My Mum said 'Look at all the things you've just written down, all the things you've ever done'. It was so obvious when you looked at it.

She could offer no examples of teachers she particularly admired but told me she wanted to teach older children and make them 'independent learners' because it reminded her of how she had been prepared, as a top junior, for secondary education. My own teaching had been similarly driven towards achieving more independent learning with younger children and although this was not a formal part of my research outline, I was keen to see how this vision developed. I had noted also that Kim was quite outspoken about wider educational issues. During the first few weeks of her course, she described open plan schools as 'nonsense'. She claimed that teachers broadly welcomed the introduction of a National Curriculum so that they could 'get it right' by teaching in a 'more traditional style' and that she thought that 'the old curriculum was absolutely ridiculous and I've never seen anything like it'. I was aware that her views were based on limited first-hand experience of education and that much of her rhetoric must have stemmed from family debate, so I was intrigued to see how these ideas developed during her training.

Kim explained that as competition for places on the course was heavy, she thought it likely that the university had identified and rejected students they believed had tried to enter the teaching profession for anything other than the 'right reasons'. Understandably, all of the beginning teachers I interviewed felt that they were on the course for the 'right reasons', while making regular references to some significant, cynical others who were not. One of the few men on the course explained to me that he had chosen primary education specifically because:

> It's wrong in a sense, you know, there are plenty of women who don't get as many promotions as the men but it is good for promotion in primary if you are a man. It's not a dead important issue but I mean it was another plus really for primary as opposed to secondary.

This student failed to complete his course.

When I asked what Kim hoped to gain personally from the course she explained that she already felt that she had the right kind of attitude and personality, and had had valid pre-course experiences in schools and simply wanted:

...someone to say to me; 'Right, this is what you've got to do, this is how you put it into practice in the classroom yourself'. I feel I need to draw together all the things I've done in the past.

My second reason for selecting Kim as a potential case study was that I was interested how which she saw the National Curriculum as likely to achieve some kind of social justice. She said: 'It ensures that people will have the same experiences to prepare them for the secondary school', and claimed that this was likely to achieve a fairer distribution of educational provision, although:

I think people get a bit stressed about topics like equality (pause). Perhaps I'm just a cynic (pause). I think people are terribly concerned about being PC and all the rest of it and I think basically it is a matter of common sense isn't it?

Having rated Kim as articulate, confident and overtly critical about some areas of educational provision, I was interested in her stated reluctance to join a 'politically correct' bandwagon to gain her qualification, and wanted to see if any elements of the course or of her experiences in schools would encourage her to reconsider her standpoint.

Finally, I was interested in the way Kim linked her personal religious beliefs to education in general and multiculturalism in particular. Just as Helen had declared herself already 'sensitive to the issues', Kim believed that she was better placed than some of her peers because she was working from a position of religious strength which influenced the way she hoped to deal with all the children in her care and made her sensitive towards other beliefs and cultures, claiming that:

I haven't been in many schools that are terribly multicultural but I presume that is just something I will have to deal with. But I don't see that as a problem for me because I have an open mind about other cultures and (pause) how to put this? I would say that (pause) I am a Christian and as a Christian I think that you perhaps (pause) because you try to act with Christian values you try to empathise with people...

When I asked Kim about the likelihood of her coming into contact with ethnic minority children during her course she acknowledged that 'knowing what (Mid)shire's like' this was unlikely. She went on to list other institutions that had 'more access to multicultural societies' and told me how it would be 'very difficult' and 'very hypocritical' for her university to begin to facilitate placements outside their immediate catchment area. So I thought that Kim would make an interesting case study on several levels. She was keen to explain any aspect of her training or her personal philosophy in detail, she had already developed a critical image of the education system before she enrolled on the course, she was articulate about her wider moral and religious philosophies and about her open-minded approach towards ethnic minorities.

Kim's predictions were proved correct with her first school experience, where she came across no ethnic minority children at all. This placement was in a rural school she frequently described as 'nice' or 'lovely'. The placement was in many ways ideal for her. She explained that there was a 'scripture union' group for staff and pupils once a week after school, that the school's policy on RE was 'broadly Christian' and that it fitted with her philosophy of 'treating everyone with respect'. She said that the school did not have a multicultural policy and that if there were an equal opportunities policy she had never seen it. Kim returned to her 'politically correct' theme when she later explained to me that when her school did cover a multicultural issue she had the impression that their rationale was: 'We are doing this about Divali because we have to do it, it is multicultural and it is politically correct'.

Although Kim was outspoken and persuasive when explaining her position on education, religion and multicultural education, I began to suspect that there was some gap between the rhetoric of her desire to be open-minded and respectful of others and the reality of her practice and professional development. For example, early in the research when she was telling me that her school explored specific religious themes such as 'determination', she remarked: 'Next week we're looking at Genghis Khan and determination. He was *very* determined'. At first I accepted such statements as at best knowing irony or at worst innocent observation, but later became convinced that there was a more worrying aspect to Kim's philosophy.

My concerns started while I was interviewing Kim during her first teaching placement. We had arranged to meet in her school, but she rang the night before to tell me she had taken sick leave. She told me she was still prepared to go ahead with the interview if I would come to her parents' home. In the interview Kim described the children in her class and told me that: 'there are a couple of stupids, but apart from that it is generally a nice school'. Towards the end of the interview I returned to this remark and asked her to elaborate. She told me that:

> It's just generally, they've got very little money, their Dad isn't their real Dad but that isn't a particular problem. They've been round loads of schools, and this is their last chance. They have had places all over the catchment area and all the rest of it (pause) they haven't got very many *clothes*, without being too horrible – they *smell*.

She went on to describe the mother of one of these children as:

> A fierce lady, very very blue eyes. Wayne's got them as well, really sort of staring and quite weird. I think that they just (pause) let them do whatever, to be honest.

Whilst it would be inappropriate to conclude that Kim (albeit subliminally) was making a direct link between intelligence and social status, it is significant that she appeared to measure her relationships with children in terms of familial wealth, the strength of their nuclear family unit, their range of acceptable clothing, their personal cleanliness and the expressions in their eyes. Later in the interview she mentioned that Wayne was receiving learning support. Having been responsible as a Deputy Head for securing the services of learning support teams I knew how stringent were the criteria by which such support is allocated, so I was surprised when Kim declared: 'He doesn't really need learning support, he can do the stuff, he's just a (pause) you know (pause) he's just messing about and all the rest of it'. As a teacher I found it difficult to accept this unsubstantiated educational statement about a pupil made by a student only a few weeks into her training but I thought that challenging her this stage would jeopardise the open and truthful way she expressed her views and thereby threaten the quality of my research.

Kim related how she had been concerned about Wayne and the imminent arrival of the university tutor to watch her teach. She had decided to 'stamp on him straight away'. What this meant was that she deliberately decided to exclude him from a class drama activity before the tutor arrived. This in turn had led to some behavioural retaliation from Wayne that happened in front of the tutor, and an eventual confrontation between the child and Kim. She told me how her tutor had suggested that: 'It would have been nice if you could have dealt more positively with him', to which she replied:

> Yes, in theory, yes it would have been lovely, however in practice (pause) (laughs). All the teachers have a problem with him and his brother because you give them chances and chances and you work with them positively and you start to build things up you know, with all the things that they've got in place ... you build them up and then they go and do something completely out of order and you just (pause) 'why bother?'.

At this point in her training, Kim seemed convinced that certain terms and attitudes were acceptable within the beginning teachers' vocabulary and seemed completely at ease using terms such as 'stupids' in an educational context.

As a researcher however, I was most concerned about Kim's final comment: 'Why bother?' Having left the classroom to examine the way in which a new generation of teachers was being trained, I found myself talking to a student who, at the start of her course, was facing important social, educational, and professional issues in her classroom and had already found refuge in the denial of 'why bother?' Kim's own rationale for this stance seemed to be her stated antipathy towards anything she perceived as 'politically correct'. This was to become another recurring theme of our discussions, evolving into a real issue for teacher educators that came to a head during the university's formal multicultural education input (recounted in Rachel's story).

I was keen to observe how these views would evolve in spite of, or even because of, the structural mechanisms employed by the university as part of Kim's training and whether there might be a clash of beliefs which would generate some critical self-examination. On the other hand, I could not help but suspect that the needs of this beginning teacher were not going to be met unless her main school experience was significantly challenging and certainly not based on the kind of comfortable relationship epitomised in Helen's school. I found myself hoping that Kim would find herself in a school where she would have to begin to confront some of her own views about children, teaching and learning in primary schools.

When we were discussing future school placements Kim told me: 'To be honest I think it is just a question of what schools they have got, and who they have got to put where'. Ironically, this proved to be true: she was contacted in advance by the university and offered a choice of an urban school-based close to the university or a rural school placed close to her own home. Naturally, she chose the latter. A senior lecturer from her university course might easily have been describing Kim when she told me that:

> We attract a fairly white, middle class, protestant type who, if you look at the application forms, particularly for the four year course, most people have got some church background, they've got an interest in children that shows itself in either Sunday school teaching or brownies or guides ... I think that we tend to attract people from a similar kind of background, fairly small town or village background. So we end up attracting a type of person who could be closed minded, in particular could be closed minded in terms of equal opportunities.

This issue has not gone unnoticed amongst writers (Cross, 1993 p64) or the beginning teachers themselves. A student from the school-based course told me: 'I don't think there is a problem with any of the people on our course, although we're all white, middle class, female'. It was interesting that other supervisors at the same university saw this social group as a positive and particularly desirable model. One of the supervising lecturers told me:

> I supervised a student the year before last whose parents were both teachers. Her father was a Headteacher and she was simply superb. Just brilliant ... she had got it all together and that was because she had come from a background of teachers.

So one can see why Kim would fall so neatly within this profile. Having identified that this is the kind of clientele the university is likely to attract, however, it seems strange that rather than challenge these preconceptions and prejudices the school placement system should validate and even strengthen them.

When I arrived to interview Kim during this second and main school experience, the supervising teacher immediately explained that most of the surrounding houses in the catchment area were in the £200,000 to £300,000 bracket. There were some ethnic minority children at the school but she was quick to point out that these were the children of airline pilots, television personalities or the 'professional classes', so there was 'no problem'. There are clear parallels here with the experiences of some of the Arts Education for a Multicultural Society (AEMS) artists who worked in these areas of the country, one of whom observed:

> It is interesting to begin to monitor people's views in (Mid)shire, ranging from overt racists to those who deny that there is a problem or an issue. In (Mid)shire, I have come across some of the most vitriolic abuse I have ever heard or seen in children's writing. There is much awareness-raising to be done. For example, I visited a non-AEMS school. In response to a question, the Headteacher said that there were no children of different ethnic backgrounds in the school. However, whilst going round the school, we saw at least three Asian children. When I asked the Head about these pupils, her reply was that these children had professional fathers (and therefore didn't count) (Robinson and Hustler, 1995 p72).

Kim felt as though she 'fitted in' immediately, telling me that she seemed to understand the ethos of the school intuitively, that they seemed to 'talk her language' and that her supervising teacher was 'really really friendly and lovely, so we get on very well'. Remembering that her first school did not have a multicultural education policy, I asked if she had been able to locate one this time. She replied: 'Equal opportunities is worked into each policy. They said they haven't got a completely separate one, it is part of each policy, so it is there. I don't know about multicultural but I imagine there is one'. About the children her class she said:

> I am very conscious that the class is brilliant because there are only 22 of them in this lovely big room and they are all (pause) well two thirds of the class are very mature and work on a high level and you say 'Can you sit with a friend' and they just do it and they work well.

Kim's supervising teacher had been teaching for six years and had spent her whole career in the same school. When I first raised the issue of multicultural education with her she at once began to talk about bullying but then insisted that the two were not connected. The second time I raised the issue of multicultural education she talked only about behaviour contracts. When I asked if multicultural education had been any part of her training provision for Kim she said it had not, and then outlined a typical 'permeation' model:

> We don't really have a problem with that at all ... We try and bring it in all across, obviously, in things like art and music and things like that but I suppose it comes out more in something like if we do some PHSE or if we do (pause) the RE it tends to come out ... Well in the RE it certainly comes through but it comes from Kim as well, I know that ... well I don't think we have really addressed it in any other curriculum area.

Clearly the teacher relies heavily on the supposition that multicultural education is 'in there somewhere', mirroring the assertions of the lecturers at the two universities. The teacher begins with the now classic misconception of linking multicultural education with 'having a problem'. The intuitive associations she makes with multicultural education are bullying and the need for behaviour contracts. She then assures me that multicultural education is brought in 'all across' the curriculum and insists that it is 'obviously' part of the school's 'art and music and things like that'. She follows this with a more tentative 'I suppose it comes out more' and then adds a conditional 'if' PHSE is done, and the stronger assertion that it takes place in RE. She is positive that it has been part of Kim's teaching even though she had stated that this had not been part of the dialogue between them, and even though Kim could not tell me how multicultural education had been any part of her planning.

Regarding the multicultural education that the supervising teacher 'knew' had come through Kim's RE lessons, Kim did not share the perception. She told me how she had focused her work on stories using her own personal Bible and was pleased that 'the children seem to have been very interested in me being so open about the fact that I am a Christian', adding that her openness 'has built up quite a nice atmosphere'. The teacher's final comment that 'I don't think we have addressed it in any other curriculum area' clearly contradicts her original belief that multicultural education was brought in 'all across' the curriculum. A deconstruction of this suggests that again there is a desire to claim that multicultural education almost naturally permeates the primary curriculum, together with the suspicion that it is not there at all.

Permeation: the invisible strategy

We saw how permeation as a model of dealing with equality issues has been discredited, and how the introduction of the National Curriculum resulted in attempts to scour the early core documentation for evidence to support the inclusion of issues such as multicultural education alongside holistic, child-centred teaching methods. My data indicates that the belief in permeation in primary schools is alive and well and that it has found its way back onto the ITE agenda:

> For the foreseeable future the context of multicultural education appears to be one of preservation and retrieval ... the strategy now has to be one of permeation of a prescribed, subject-based curriculum, whatever the difficulties involved, and however much this may reduce the potential effect (Grinter, 1994 p166).

Grinter asserts that 'there is no question about the legitimacy of multicultural education in the National Curriculum' (1994 p162), and has outlined ways in which the subject can be incorporated into the programmes of study at Key Stage Two (Grinter 1994, 1995, 1997). A comparable exercise has been undertaken by other writers (King *et al.*, 1993, Manning, 1997) and by the National Union of Teachers (NUT, 1996). After denouncing them in earlier writing, Iram Siraj-Blatchford has re-assessed her stance on permeation models for ITE (Siraj-Blatchford, 1994 pp149-165), and others have called for a model of permeation which evolves out of compulsory staff development (Clay and George, 1993 p132). However, this appears to be a move made in desperation, as though in recognition that the current climate can permit a permeation model of multicultural education or nothing at all. Even this limited optimism does not sit easily with my data, nor with

Swann's concern lest permeation be 'just a paper promise' (DES, 1985 p559), nor with Gaine's warning that 'things can become so well permeated that they disappear altogether' (Gaine, 1988 p171). Nor does it fit with the conclusion that 'permeation as a model for change cannot work whilst it is being 'implemented' by people who have not raised their own consciousness and understanding of issues of race and racism' (ARTEN, 1988 p4).

Others have found that primary teachers do not perceive issues such as multicultural education to be part of their training brief with beginning teachers (Ball, 1987, Radnor, 1997). The teachers I interviewed placed all their emphasis on classroom management and the effective delivery of the National Curriculum, seeing issues such as multicultural education as the responsibility of the university, and a 'theoretical' issue best dealt with in formal lectures. Typical responses during my research were:

> It's the job of the college. They've got enough staff, it's their job. Let's be honest here, who's getting their training done on the cheap? It's their job. I have never dealt with things like multicultural education with a student. It's not really an issue here anyway but it's the college who should be doing it (Supervising teacher on university-based course).

> There is nothing to address, really. Nothing at all...The tendency on teaching practice is you address things as they arise don't you? You say 'What do I do in this situation?' and you address it like that, so it's just not there (Mentor on school-based course).

> Multicultural education I don't think you learn in school, that's where you need the experience at university. Things like that. The social and moral side of things are better taught at the university because you don't see it unless you are told about it, and then you can say 'Oh yes, I've seen that now', but here you don't see it. At all. I mean we have one Caribbean child and one sort of Asian child and that's it. You just don't see it. You don't come across it (Supervising teacher on university-based course).

Only one supervising teacher or mentor told me how he actively made multicultural education an issue with the beginning teachers in his care. He articulated a wider philosophy of education which incorporated a personal sense of social justice and a commitment to ensure that all beginning teachers who came into contact with him considered issues of inequality and disadvantage. It may be significant that this teacher was the most outspoken supporter of school-based ITE, stating: 'It's turning out bloody good teachers. It's much better than the old system. This is the future, I'm convinced of it'. All the other teachers and mentors thought it unrealistic to deal with issues such as multicultural education in schools, and that it was ultimately the responsibility of the university to ensure that these issues were dealt with. Most of them cast doubt on the need for multicultural education at all in their all-white areas of the country.

Developing categories for children

Remembering Kim's teacher's comments about the school's ethnic minority population, I asked about the ethnic minority children in her class. Kim replied:

> Kamala is from an Asian family. Her parents are (pause) I can't remember (pause) lawyers, doctors, (pause) but they are very special people. Shahid is (pause) not really black but I suppose that he's (pause) he's got coloured skin anyway. I think he's fostered at the moment. And Chris is from a black family as well. He's gorgeous. All bright eyed and bushy tailed.

An analysis of this description suggests a good deal. It could be argued that Kim demonstrates several misconceptions about these children, beginning with an accommodation of ethnic identity within a 'treat them all the same' philosophy which dovetails neatly with her 'Christian empathy with people'. Kim thinks that she can disregard Kamala's ethnic identity because the child has professional parents. She need not even remember their precise occupations because she knows that they are 'very special people'. Shahid's ethnic identity, too, can be disregarded, as he is 'not really black', although Kim qualifies this by acknowledging that he does have 'coloured skin'. It is interesting that Kim makes the distinction between having 'coloured skin' and being black. Having found a conceptual way around recognising the ethnic status of two of the three ethnic minority children in her class, she then appears to distance the third. Just as she shows no understanding of ethnic identity in her distanced description of Kamala as being from an Asian family, Kim offers the observation that Chris is 'from a black family' instead of saying he is black, qualifying this further with the description of him as 'gorgeous' and 'bright eyed and bushy tailed'.

Kim was not the only one who seemed to want to dismiss ethnicity in predominantly white classrooms. Several similar incidents occurred during my data collection, two of which demonstrate an almost institutionalised process. In the smallest school I visited there were fewer than eighty children. Before videotaping a piece of drama developed by one of my sample group, I had arranged an interview with the Head, and when I asked about equal opportunities and multicultural education he told me:

> In this school, to be honest with you I don't see as we have any problem. A) we have nobody from other cultures to be honest with you, but B) the equal opportunities side, I think I'm the one who has to worry about that here. I'm the only man here (laughs). I'm the only one that's harassed here. But there's no problem about that ... here, we don't differentiate at all.

When I went into the student's class to start filming I was surprised to see a black boy in the room. When I asked the student about him I was even more surprised to learn that he had a sister in the lower class. Arriving at another school for a student and teacher interview, the first person I saw was a white boy sitting silently and cross-legged underneath a table outside the Head's office. I registered my arrival with the secretary, who told me I could use the staffroom where I would not be interrupted, and led me out past the boy, who was still under the table but was now talking to his black friend. At interview the student informed me that there were no ethnic minority children in the school, which I found surprising as of the two pupils I had seen, I knew one was black. I interviewed the supervising teacher immediately afterwards, who confirmed what the student had said:

Russell	You haven't got many ethnic minority children in this school have you?
Teacher	No.
Russell	Are there any at all?
Teacher	We had one lad who is Muslim, so (pause) it doesn't really apply to us.

When I went into the student's classroom there, at the back of the room was an Asian girl in shalwar-kamise and burkha. These observations make strange, uneasy reading and I realise that I could not have invented a sharper illustration of how ethnicity is treated with a conspiracy of silence in certain predominantly white primary schools. Surely one cannot presume that there is an unspoken, common drive among beginning teachers, experienced classroom teachers and Headteachers to seek equality in their schools through a 'pretence' that the children were not black. But if we reject this deconstruction, we then have to believe that these professionals had genuinely not noticed the ethnicity of the children.

These visual 'disappearances' and textual 'silences' seemed to typify approaches made by the many educators who appeared to eliminate ethnic identity from their perceptions of the ethnic minority children in their care. My field work suggests that this was how many beginning teachers sought to conceptualise the issue of ethnicity. My data revealed no examples of a clearer understanding about race. Instead of openly exploring what was meant by multi-cultural education or race, my interview subjects repeatedly found ways to avoid dealing with the subject, and took refuge in silence.

By categorising children as 'not really black', by insisting that professional parental status in some way cancelled out ethnic identity, by allowing cleaners to use racist language unchecked in front of children and parents, by allowing racist graffiti to remain in place outside the school gates, by maintaining the pretence that racial violence was not an issue for *'our* children' even when there were incidents of it in the school, by refusing to talk about ethnic issues in case the talk itself creates a problem that wasn't there before, by dismissing first-hand evidence of members of ethnic communities, by finding solace in a conception of themselves as 'sensitive' and 'already converted', and by maintaining the belief that *'somebody else* deals with these issues so that absolves *me* of responsibility', these voices forge a formidable silence which characterised my entire investigation. These silences become even more ominous in light of the research from Gillborn and Gipps (1996) suggesting that 'failure to address ethnic diversity has proved counter-productive' and that there is evidence of growing conflict between white teachers and African-Caribbean children where, 'despite their best intentions, teachers' actions can create and amplify conflict' (reported in Rafferty, 1996 p3).

Returning to Kim, I could not help noticing a connection between her assessment and description of the ethnic minority children in her class and her earlier perception of Wayne. Kim referred to Shahid as 'quite bright but in a weird sort of way' (echoing her assessment of Wayne). About the three children however, Kim only went into any detail about Kamala:

> Kamala is (pause) she is a funny girl. She is very little, she is very emotionally immature. She is very very behind the others. It is like having a Year Three. They think that (pause) partly that (pause) the school are wondering now if there is something wrong because she is getting further and further behind. She is quite intelligent, the work she has done has been fine, it is just her attitude ... she plays at being very small and very frightened but she is actually very manipulative. She does daft things, she just (pause) you can stand there and tell her off and you can give her a real ticking off and she skips back to her seat.

Deconstructing Kim's assessment of Kamala could suggest that there are several issues to be explored about Kamala's experience of school. Just as Kim made a distinction between the school's assessment of Wayne's ability and her own, implying that her perception was keener and more professionally astute, she knows best also about Kamala. It is the school who is wondering if there is something wrong, but despite the 'fact' that Kamala is falling behind the others in her class, Kim can see that this is not related to her ability as she is 'quite intelligent', and that 'the work she has done has been fine'. For Kim, Kamala's lack of success is due to the child's attitude, echoing her assessment of Wayne as not really needing learning support: 'he can do the stuff ... he's just messing about'.

I found myself intrigued also with Kim's account of Terry, a white boy in her class. Kim reported that he had recently moved into the area from the Moss Side region of Manchester, and although details of his recent past were sketchy it was clear that his mother had left home, and that Terry had moved into some local council-owned property and his father was not comfortable dealing with schools. Kim observed that Terry's father seemed to be 'making a real effort because (Terry) came in the following week with a school jumper and he had *never had a school jumper before!*' and described how Terry had asked about the dates for the half term break so that his father could make some personal arrangements, telling me that:

> The Dad came into school to tell the secretary (pause) and he had never been into school before and we were all cowering because (laughs) Mr Meakin's come in!!

I could not help but remember the serendipitous moment outside Helen's classroom that changed the route of my research, and wonder how it might have changed again had I been present at Mr Meakin's visit. There were echoes of our earlier conversations when she began to talk about Terry's disruption to the rest of the class and his inappropriate behaviour. She used her earlier terminology: 'I mean people like Terry who come from a bit of a (pause) who come from a rough background that are just downright *stupid*'. Again, I am not claiming that Kim makes some uncomplicated association between social class and intelligence but it was impossible for me to ignore the number of times she raised the two issues within the same sentence. Talking about Terry obviously evoked memories of Wayne and she began to reminisce:

> Looking back he was an absolute nightmare. The thing was you had to keep reminding yourself that it wasn't all his fault, but he was so vicious and so manipulative and horrible ... I think Wayne should have been in a special unit with his brother to be honest. I think they were trying to move things that way. But he just (pause) for the rest of the class he would just spoil it completely and it was awful because you would get to the middle of the day and inside you would really be hating that child and you just had to stop yourself so much and think 'He is only eight, he may seem like the *devil's child* but he is only eight', you know (laughs).

Significant similarities and shifts are noticeable within this statement. At first I presumed that Kim had reconsidered her position with hindsight and was prepared to admit that Wayne needed some kind of educational support, but on reflection it seemed to be more of an appeal to remove the child from her classroom. Kim readily dismissed the work already done by the school, even though she had only completed ten weeks of her initial teacher education, and she seemed far less concerned about the needs of Terry or Wayne and his brother than about her own. As a teacher I had sufficient experience of students in Kim's position, faced with a non-compliant child, to know that 'spoiling it for the rest of the class' is usually a thinly disguised 'spoiling things for me'. Thus, when Kim looks back at her relationship with Wayne, a child who did not co-operate readily, she describes him as 'an absolute nightmare', 'vicious', 'manipulative', 'horrible', 'the devil's child' and for the first time admits to feeling hatred.

The interesting elements of Kim's experience in school for me were, therefore, her relationships with the children who did not comply with her comfortable conception of teacher and learner, those who did not fit comfortably within her conception of the boundaries operating within her classroom. In real terms this meant Wayne, Terry and Kamala, all of whom she consistently referred to in exasperated, disparaging terms.

Finally, and significantly, Kim was well aware of the limitations of her practice and the implications this had for her future employment. She had no intention of working in an urban-based school or one that was culturally diverse, explaining that 'there would be little point in me applying for that sort of post because I wouldn't do it well, so it seems silly to inflict myself on children when I am not going to do a good job'. At the end of her course Kim remained vague about her understanding of educational disadvantage; nothing had happened to convince her that she should think otherwise. She still defined educational disadvantage as 'It could be anything couldn't it? I mean you could be looking at someone who is not particularly good in their subject like I wasn't very good at maths ... in a way you can pick out every child in your class and say they are disadvantaged'. Statements such as this, made by students who are days away from qualifying as primary teachers indicate an absolute lack of understanding about issues of social justice for which the training process needs to take full responsibility.

When I asked about the possibility of ethnicity being a disadvantage, Kim replied 'I mean if you are someone who is coming from somewhere very different, I mean like as in a different country, then yes it *would* be a disadvantage'. When I asked about multicultural education in predominantly white areas of the country, she laughed and said 'There's not a lot you can do about it is there? That's how it is ... it just boils down to having an understanding of and a respect of other people's beliefs. Whether you believe them or not'.

When, at the end of our final interview, I asked Kim for her perceptions of my research, she thought I had been looking at gender issues, and stated that equal opportunities 'really hasn't been an issue for me'. One question I asked each student at the end of their course was 'Was there any point during your training when you felt you were challenged either personally or professionally?', the intention being to afford the student the opportunity to critically reflect on aspects of their own professional development. Kim could recall no such instances. When I elaborated and asked about any critical moments during the course, she told me that the only time she ever felt challenged on any issue was when she was dealing with SATs, and declared that: 'I haven't changed my point of view on anything'. When Kim had qualified and found a teaching post I spoke to her supervising tutor at the university who told me that Kim had been assessed as 'superb', 'exceptional', 'brilliant' and 'One of the best students I've had. Ever'.

Kim's story illustrates the way in which responsibility for raising issues of social justice were systematically ignored by all participants in the training process. Kim's strongly held personal beliefs are understandable and almost predictable in their naiveté. What is less understandable is that no-one questioned how appropriate these views were in primary education, nor did anyone seek to encourage Kim to consider how her views might impact on children in her class. In effect, Kim's training achieved little more than validation of her initial position on race and social class.

The course relied on the student to somehow assimilate all the subtle component elements of social justice which permeated through the year in order for her to qualify as a rounded, well-informed and sensitive professional. When Kim is able to state that she has no intention of being employed to deal with working class or black children we have to accept that this has not been a successful strategy.

'Permeation' as experienced by Kim was no more than avoidance of the issues. The term was a conceptual crutch; something to lean against when challenged about issues not covered directly by National Curriculum legislation. My data indicates that permeation did not work as a strategy for dealing with race issues either at the level of the school or the university. Students like Kim were allowed to spend their entire training period learning how to avoid having to deal with issues fundamental to the process of effective teaching and learning.

School-based training again provokes specific issues related to race. When Kim's teacher states that she does not think of a child as black because his father is an airline pilot, the question one wants to ask is 'What would the child's father have to do before you do think of him as black?' The teacher makes the direct connection between social status and there being 'a problem', intimating that should the child's father not be an airline pilot there might well be a 'problem' (this concept resurfaces in Laura's story). Kim's own preconceptions and biases were legitimated by the school. Her insistence that she 'fitted in' immediately, and that the school seemed to 'talk her language' is worrying, but even more alarming is the realisation that the university conceived of this as a positive aspect of the training. Initially, I was surprised that I should be able to uncover these prejudices so easily while they went apparently unnoticed by members of the university, but I was to discover how this happens in practice (see Rachel's story). If racial justice is to be part of the agenda for newly qualified teachers then there needs to be some point where preconceptions about issues such as social class, race and gender are openly sought and acted upon by supervising tutors.

It may seem strange that so much of this chapter has been taken up with references to students discussing white children, but this is an important aspect of the way in which race is dealt with as a (non)issue in the white highlands. Kim's attitude towards Wayne and Terry is clearly a direct result of her own personal preconception and bias. The assumptions she makes about ability and suitability take into account parental income, marital status, clothing and hygiene. In short, she makes negative claims about children who do not fit comfortably with her notion of what a child should be like. Consequently she can accommodate black children in her classroom as long as they match her desired social status (and even then she will not acknowledge their ethnic status). Any thoughts of having to work with disadvantaged children, working class children or (taking Kamala's experience into account) black children are dismissed with the openly stated intention of not working in schools these children are likely to attend. In stating that she *would not apply* for a job in a school where there are black children, Kim communicates not only her assumptions about multi-ethnic schools but also her reluctance to challenge her own ignorance and arrogance. Teacher training in the 'white highlands' is more open to responses of this nature from the students they attract, and therefore has greater responsibility to educate their students to overcome such stereotypical and narrow views.

Chapter 5

Laura's Story
learning to teach racism

L aura had studied educational psychology as part of her first
degree so she had had more experience of being in schools
than most of her colleagues on the university-based course.
She told me that she had always wanted to teach and that she was
looking forward to being able to develop her skills as a beginning
teacher towards eventually working as an educational psychologist.
During our first interview we discussed educational inequality and
she told me that:

> When I was doing educational psychology I did a report on the com-
> parison between educational services, and one school I went into was in
> a sort of disadvantaged area and it was horrendous (pause). A child had
> been expelled from eight different schools and they didn't have the
> advantage of the parents reinforcing the learning they'd had during the
> day, the parents just didn't care about them. That's my idea of dis-
> advantage.

Laura also made the point that she felt equality issues were closely
linked to individual curriculum areas, particularly in primary
schools. She suggested design and technology as a subject where
gender issues might be raised and RE as providing teachers with
the chance to look more closely at 'culture'. She went on to say that
she considered the National Curriculum as a good example of how
inequality as an issue had been tackled:

> You know, you've got to do more than one religion. I think it has leant
> itself more towards equality than it has towards inequality ... It has made

them feel as though people respect their religion. You know (pause) there is nothing worse than going in to a school and being taught Christianity and when you go home you're a Hindu. It's (pause) you know (pause) I think it makes people (pause) especially children, have a more enlightened view of life.

She concluded:

I think the inequalities of gender and cultural issues have been excellently covered by the National Curriculum but the special needs differences (pause). It needs to go a lot further.

Encounters with social disadvantage

Having started work in school on her first attachment Laura expressed concern that some of the teachers seemed to be insensitive to the social backgrounds of some of the children. She told me that:

You sit there in the staffroom and there is nothing more annoying than (pause) we went in on Monday and there was this little lad in the school (pause) I can't remember what his name is, but he's six and his mother doesn't care about him. She sent him to school in a shirt that looked like it was her boyfriend's shirt. He was found wandering around with his little three year old sister who had fallen in the pond and he had to look after her and he didn't know what to do because his mother had gone off somewhere. I know she's in hospital having another baby. I can understand why the teacher's getting annoyed with her and saying she is selfish and all the rest of it, but when I walked in the staff room the teacher said this little lad's collar was out here, it was so huge, this shirt, his sleeves were rolled up and the teacher said 'Have you seen so and so's shirt today?' and the other teacher said 'Why, what colour is it today?' and that really infuriates me because it is not that child's fault. You don't have to get so personal about a six year old. That's what I don't want to happen. I don't want to be influenced by that. I don't want to slag off children because at the end of the day it's not that little lad's fault he's dressed like that.

Laura's concerns were significant, as they set an agenda that became confused over the course of her initial teacher education. She exhibited a simplistic desire to aspire towards some form of social justice, but the inadequacies of her training gave her no opportunities or capability to theorise about the wider meanings and educational implications of issues such as race and social class. Her conception of educational disadvantage was based heavily on parents who 'just didn't care' about their children. She saw disadvantage in simplistic terms, as a lack of parental interest characterised by inappropriate or grubby clothing. Laura talked emotively about being 'infuriated' and about not wanting 'to slag off children' and discussed the need for respect and equality, suggesting that teachers should look to the National Curriculum to apprise themselves of these issues. For her the issues of race and gender were no longer on the educational agenda as they had been dealt with 'excellently' by the National Curriculum. The issue was now one of 'respect' for individual children and how to put into practice the positive example set by the National Curriculum.

It is at this point that one can see where a more carefully structured social induction for beginning teachers into school life would be beneficial. Rather than the 'throwing them in at the deep end' approach described in Helen's story, it would surely be helpful if issues such as those outlined by Laura had been discussed at her university before she experienced them first hand in the classroom and staff room. I was repeatedly informed by teachers that they felt students 'got a better idea of the real job of teaching' during their time working on school experience, but discussions in Laura's first staff room indicate that some detailed preparation is needed before that 'reality' is experienced. It is specifically this undergraduate good-intentioned naiveté that provoked calls for initial teacher education to 'confront the moral dilemmas of teaching in a more deliberate fashion' (Liston and Zeichner, 1987 p7) but again there was no indication that challenges and explorations of this kind were part of any dialogue between beginning teachers and their mentors in school.

Laura's main placement was in a school on the outskirts of a built-up area where, she reported, there were 'quite a few' ethnic minority children. As I was able to observe a whole school assembly, 'quite a few' meant that each class contained, at most, one or two children who could be considered as having ethnic minority backgrounds. Laura was told that she could attend staff meetings but that it would 'not really be worth it'. Over the nine weeks of her placement she worked in two parallel classes, spending the first three weeks in one, and the remaining six weeks with the supervising teacher responsible for her practice. This teacher, Annette, was in her late fifties and had begun teaching in army schools but had spent virtually all her professional career at the same school. Despite her seniority and experience, Annette had not been given the responsibility of a student before. Laura perceived her as 'Very powerful, very disciplined, very organised, if you don't fit in with it then 'tough'', but she also described her experience in Annette's class as 'Heaven'. These two comments seemed to typify Laura's attachment to the school. She would readily and regularly criticise Annette for being unapproachable or confrontational but, equally, she admired her as a teacher for her strong-minded, disciplinarian approach in the classroom. Of the six weeks Laura spent in Annette's class, three were on her own, as her teacher took sick leave and left Laura with the class and a full timetable.

As usual, I asked for the school's policy on equal opportunities or multicultural education and was told that the school did not have one at present. Laura explained that the school was due for an OFSTED inspection and the staff were 'trying to get them reeled off at the moment'. I asked if she knew whether there had been a policy at her previous school and she replied 'Not that I ever saw, but then (pause) I didn't need (pause) I didn't go and look for it'.

There was one ethnic minority boy in each of the two parallel classes; Assan and Steven. While in school interviewing Laura, I noticed that the two boys were very differently perceived by both the student and the teacher. Laura first talked about Assan, who was in her current class, telling me that:

> (He) gets some terrible stick. He is a Pakistani lad and he is always crying. You know, he can't really speak very good English anyway (pause) he gets very upset and the kids call him 'Paki', but what? (silence)

I asked what happens about this and I was told:

> Nothing. They say he is as bad as they are...it really upset me when I first started because he was getting quite upset and these kids were right little nasty pieces of work.

Laura described how she had seen other children call Assan names and deliberately provoke him, then 'play innocent' to the teachers when they were questioned. She told me: 'I said 'Assan, just ignore them, you know you are worth more than them' and all that, but he still gets it now'. She went on to say that there seemed to be some doubt about whether Assan would attend the class residential trip in July, as his mother did not want him to go, whereas his father was keen that he did. Laura was aware that this might be directly related to 'the fact that he is abused, you know, racially abused', then added: 'He does give as good back. He's a little pain'.

Laura described Steven, (the boy in the second of her parallel classes) as being 'Afro-Caribbean'. She told me he was:

> More socially adept (pause) he gets on a lot better with the children than the other one does. The other one, I don't think he's got any social skills because he can't speak English properly anyway. Whereas Steven, he's straight in there with the other kids; 'Come on we're going to play soccer' and you know, he's loved by the other children.

These statements reveal several processes at work. Laura is in no doubt about what is happening in her classroom. At first she calls it 'terrible stick', she then calls it 'abuse', then immediately redefines it as 'racial abuse'. It is noticeable and significant that when Laura goes into a discussion about Steven, Assan loses his identity in the discourse, being twice referred to as 'the other one'. She explains that she has witnessed not only how Assan has been racially abused but also how his abusers have managed to avoid any repercussions, yet she is unable to deal with the situation other than to tell Assan that he is 'worth more than them'. This cannot be much comfort for Assan. Firstly he has the reality of the abuse to deal with. Secondly he has been made to realise that the abusers have no regard for the sanctuary of the classroom but attack him unchecked in front of the adult in charge of the class. This means that, thirdly, he has the indignity of knowing that his teacher has tacitly condoned the abusers' actions. Finally he is all too aware that the outcome of this knowledge is that he will have to face precisely the same kind of abuse again in the future. As Laura herself acknowledges: 'he still gets it now'.

Blaming the victim

It is interesting to examine how Laura appears to have come to terms with this situation personally, and moreover, has entered dangerous ground where she even seems to find justification for the repeated abuse by the 'right little nasty pieces of work', by putting some of the blame on Assan himself. She relates how she was 'really upset' by these incidents 'when I first started', but implies that she no longer is – firstly through her implicit justification of the abuse, secondly because, as she twice points out, this is partly because 'he can't speak very good English anyway', and thirdly because he has no, in her view, 'social skills' and, unlike Steven, is not 'loved by the other children'. Finally, she takes refuge in the claim that 'He does give as good back. He's a little pain'. Laura's statements thus indicate that although she clearly understands the abuse to be both persistent and of a racial nature, she is not only unwilling to confront the issue but also wants to excuse the abuse and then blame the child for his own social 'weaknesses'. This sits uneasily with Laura's earlier concerns about 'respect' and her dismay over the six year old boy in the big shirt being 'slagged off' by his teachers. It sits even more uneasily with her earlier description of her time in the school as 'Heaven'.

The perceived understanding of racism, substantiated by Macpherson's report on the Stephen Lawrence Inquiry, is that it remains powerful and pervasive, but that it can operate much more subtly. There seems no such subtlety in Assan's experience in school. For the children in this class, racism is a taught experience. The abuse Assan faces is real, frequent and takes numerous forms. His peers not only witness this on a regular basis inside and outside the classroom, but are taught by two adults who are seen to condone this behaviour. Racism is thus effectively a taught and learnt process incorporating regular demonstrations and conceptual reinforcement for an entire class of children.

When I asked if Steven was also abused by the other children, Laura laughed and said: 'They wouldn't dare give it to him. He is very respected by the other children. Very respected'. She then referred back to Assan, saying that he:

...can't mix properly with the other children. He just can't ... you see him looking at children dead longingly and it is really sad, because he can't mix with them, it's just sad.

When I again asked what was being done about this, Laura replied that the teacher told her to just 'watch and don't take everything he says', and 'don't take any notice of him, he gives as much back'. Thus Annette's instructions supported the stance taken by Laura and indicated that Assan's situation was unlikely to improve during his time with her. Although I did not want to create any tensions between the teachers and learners involved in my study, and although I had not asked this question directly of any other student, I felt I had to tackle Annette's advice more openly, so I asked Laura if she felt that Annette's behaviour might be interpreted as in any way racist. She replied:

No, I wouldn't, because she likes Steven, but I think that is because he works well. Steven is the one who everybody loves. He is a lovely lad, you know and Assan can drive you mad at times because he'll go (affects accent) 'Oh Miss' and he'll mumble stuff to you and you'll go 'What? I can't hear you', and then when he is participating in class he seems as though he doesn't understand what you are talking about, but when he produces his written work he does! I think he just lacks social skills, Assan. It's quite sad.

It is interesting that Laura defended her teacher in this way and that she further qualifies the distinctions she has established between the two boys. Again several issues are raised for which there are no simple explanations. Possibly Assan does not comply with Laura's conception of 'disadvantage' because he shows no physical evidence of parental neglect and so does not fit her category of disadvantage. Perhaps Laura does not want to acknowledge the racism in Assan's situation (despite having admitted that this is so), because for her issues of race have been dealt with 'excellently' by the National Curriculum. If Laura's teacher is able to deal with Assan's abuse by ignoring it, and the National Curriculum somehow deals with racism effectively, then Laura can again remove herself from the responsibility of tackling the issue herself despite the reality that the children are being taught powerful lessons about social justice.

Laura's understanding of racism seems shaky: she felt that she could not be racist if there was a black child she liked. When I asked if there had been any ethnic minority children in Laura's previous school, she replied that there had been one, and then described him as a 'nightmare' and a 'little monster'. She went on:

> He was a right little swine. It was nothing to do with his colour because I am not racist (pause) but he used it as an excuse. Do you know what I mean?

Realising that there seemed to be some discrepancy between the distress she had witnessed with Assan and the lack of direction offered by her supervising teacher, I asked Laura to tell me in detail about the discussions she had with Annette about the children in her class, and she told me:

> She says things to me like 'Well you see him now, he's as thick as pig shit' and I think 'Don't get involved' because I get really (pause) I've been told off by one of my tutors for this, for trying to think that you can have success with every child (pause) She says 'I'll tell you what' she says 'For the first few weeks I'll put you with the thickos', and it is that sort of attitude and I really don't like it.

Laura later explained that this conversation took place on the first observation day before she began her attachment. She recalled the incident:

> We went swimming in the afternoon. She said 'You can come swimming if you want'. We went in for observation on the Thursday and the Friday, and we were due to start on the Monday and she said 'Oh we've got an odd bunch' and this kid was swimming past and she just went 'See him there, all I can say is that he is as thick as pig shit'.

Laura mentioned a disabled boy in the class who, she claimed, was perceived by Annette as exploiting his disability at every possible occasion. She advised Laura:

> I don't think we should do anything about it, because it will only cause confrontation. Let him pick and choose. Let him choose his own path in life.

When I returned to the subject of this child in our final interview, Laura told me that she had expressed concerned about this boy's progress and had been told:

> Just ignore it, don't confront the parents whatever you do, just let him go along with whatever he wants to do, he'll fall behind and it will be his own fault.

I asked if this was indicative of the way Annette perceived Assan. Laura replied:

> Yes, I think it is. It is just 'So what? I'll just get my job done and that will be it'. Do you know what I mean? And those who want to work well are wonderful children, and those who don't (pause). It's their problem, let them sort it out.

Remembering Kim's remark: 'Why bother?' along with Helen's helplessness and her bewildered: 'What do you say?', this data begins to present a disturbing picture. If we bring together all these comments:

> Just ignore it
>
> Don't get involved
>
> It will be his own fault
>
> It's their problem, let them sort it out
>
> I don't think we should do anything about it, because it will only cause confrontation

– all made in reference to the most disadvantaged children in these classes – serious questions arise for the people who are responsible for educating beginning teachers. Similarly, descriptions of children as 'thickos' and 'as thick as pig shit' do nothing to lift the aspirations of those entering the profession, nor do they indicate that these people should have the privilege of educating new entrants merely because they are teachers.

Laura criticised Annette for taking the stance that 'I'll just get my job done and that will be it', and yet this seems to be precisely the (racist) lesson that Laura has learned. In many ways, this situation mirrors the research into conflict during teaching practice which identified the dominant student ploy of 'strategic compliance' (Sparkes and Mackay, 1996 p18), but there were also moments of considerable congruence. On the one hand, Laura felt unable to question Annette's professional judgement and resigned herself to merely getting through her school experience, but on the other hand the practice of teacher and student merged at certain points, such as in their conception and treatment of Assan and their readiness to put the blame back on him for his lack of social success and for the abuse he suffered. Similarly, any shortcomings in the performance of the disabled boy were seen to be his own fault, as both teacher and student chose to leave the boy to his own devices.

Readers should remember that none of these incidents were discussed with the student's university tutor.

When I asked Annette for an interview she told me curtly that she would give me five minutes but that she was very busy. We went into the staffroom where another member of staff was working. I gave a brief outline of my research, which was received with cold acceptance. I then sketched my professional history as a primary teacher and Deputy Head, to which Annette visibly warmed. I began by asking her to describe the school's social mix and she replied: 'Well I don't think you would call it Tory heartland'. The other member of staff added 'You could put Mickey Mouse up for Labour and he'd get in'. Annette replied 'Yes. There are a lot of special needs'.

Hoping to bring the conversation around to Assan and remembering that he had difficulties with his spoken English, I asked about EAL (English as an Additional Language) provision in the school. She immediately mentioned Steven, (whose English was perfect), stating:

> His father is from Mauritius and his mother is Filipino but I don't know what they talk at home. I would think English because father is a clinical psychologist, he's not stupid at all.

I tried to bring the conversation back to children who had specific language needs, but again Annette spoke only of Steven. At no stage did she mention Assan, despite the fact that the boy was a member of her class and that Laura had repeatedly insisted that 'he can't speak English properly'.

A deconstruction of this exchange brings several issues into sharp relief. Annette appears to maintain an unproblematic relationship whereby Assan is somehow subsumed within Steven. Although Assan has difficulties with spoken English, this can be ignored as an issue of ethnicity because Steven's English is perfect, thus the blame and the responsibility for change rests solely with Assan. Although Assan is regularly mocked by the other children, this can be ignored as the children 'love' and 'respect' Steven. Again this can be perceived as Assan's responsibility and not as an issue of ethnicity. It is interesting that Annette and Laura both found other ways to conceptualise and dismiss ethnicity. Kim's supervising teacher felt able to dismiss ethnic identity because of parental occupation, and here is Annette engaging in the same process and taking it still further. Initially, it would seem that Annette simply dismisses Steven's ethnic identity because his father is a clinical psychologist, but she adds the qualification that 'he's not stupid at all'. This seems to imply firstly that it is natural to expect members of ethnic minority groups to be stupid, secondly that intelligence is measured by the ability to speak English, and thirdly that Assan is conceptually dismissable because he qualifies (for her) within the categories of black, stupid and unable to speak English.

Laura seemed unaware of the issues she and her supervising teacher generated. As far as she was concerned there was only the issue of the individual child. The child was the issue, not racism, because the child did not seem to want to make the effort to learn the language, to be sociable, to play football, to be loved by the other children. In our final meeting, when we reminisced about incidents she had experienced in school, Laura still believed that the National Curriculum brought about a state of equality in the classroom and added: 'I think multicultural issues are not the sort of thing you address today'. As a newly qualified teacher, Laura thinks that the National Curriculum is a vehicle by which equality can be achieved in the classroom, while at the same time supposing that this happens without issues such as multicultural education being tackled – she perceives this as an outdated issue that no longer needs attention. When I asked her to be more specific about this issue and to illustrate exactly what she meant, she alluded only to the National Curriculum's reference to clothing in PE.

Perhaps these statements merely reflect Laura's inexperience. De-tailed scrutiny of the data, however, suggests that they are more likely to be an indication of her inability to conceive of and arti-culate a wider social philosophy about teaching as a profession. In our final interview at the end of Laura's course, I thought of her initial enthusiasm for the job and asked her to define the role of the teacher. She replied:

> Erm (pause). I don't know because (pause). My philosophy of teaching is still the same, but you find that your role as a teacher, when you are actually in practice, especially when you are working with other people, is their philosophy, working within their philosophy and I would say (pause). Well, from what I've done so far, it's basically to teach, and that's it.

If we consider her reply in the context of wider learning about race issues on initial teacher education courses in predominantly white areas, it provides a vivid example of how one student could not conceptualise the issue in any way beyond that of the naïve individual. She conceived of the issue as one which had been dealt with at national level, and now no longer needed to be addressed by herself, the class teacher or the school's policies. It was Assan's own responsibility, in effect, to be more like Steven.

Small wonder then that beginning teachers are unable to articulate a philosophy of education, or even their conceptions about teachers and learners, beyond the technical organisation, delivery and assessment of practical materials. They are being educated in a climate which devalues the teacher's professional voice. Without disputing the need for a nationally agreed curriculum which co-ordinates learning and brings some form of working structure to state education, the pace of legislation, lack of consultation and the emphasis on reporting, testing and formal school inspections has clearly undermined the professional status of educators.

Never mind the theory

The establishment of new routes into the profession has also weakened the professional status of teachers (Lunt *et al.*, 1993). The introduction of non-graduates in the form of licensed teachers and the articled teacher scheme characterised the shift of emphasis towards 'on the job' training at the 'chalk face' and the devaluing of 'theory-based' education. The approach was epitomised by (then) Secretary of State John Patten's proposals for a 'Mum's army', whereby non-graduates would achieve teacher status in infant schools after completing a twelve month, largely classroom-based course. It is widely recognised that legislation over recent years has been directed by documents published by New Right think tanks (see Ball, 1990, Hill, 1994a, Tomlinson, 1996). One such document enquired:

> Is there any evidence that the theoretical studies of education under-taken in formal teacher training, as opposed to the studies of one's sub-ject and the teaching practice, actually help to make better teachers? (O'Hear, 1988 p20).

O'Hear went on to suggest that a curriculum which tackled inequalities in practice usually meant a curriculum which was watered down to suit the less than equal (O'Hear, 1988 p22). Another New Right thinker was quoted as saying:

> Teachers with Cert. Ed. after their names have studied nonsense for 3 years. Those with B.Ed 3 or 4 years. Those with PGCE have had a break for one year studying nonsense after they had done a proper subject and those with M.Ed or Adv.Dip.Ed have returned for super nonsense (Anderson, 1982 p11).

As those in the teaching profession have precisely these qualifications it is hardly surprising that they have become increasingly devalued. The government's intervention into initial teacher education to 'rectify' this matter by seeking to control over content and method at Higher Education Institution (HEI) level has left interested onlookers in little doubt about the direction ITE is going (Tysome, 1996c p3). When the (outgoing) Secretary of State for Education was asked if she thought there was still a place for educational theory as traditionally taught by university education departments, she replied:

> I certainly think the balance is switching, and probably rightly, to skills and competencies (sic) in the classroom. I am sure that is right. I think that education theory, of course, is important as background, but it's not much help on a wet and windy Friday afternoon with class 4B (Gillian Shephard interviewed in Ribbins and Sherratt, 1997 p225).

Statements such as this have provoked criticism. Professor New-bold has argued that 'The initial training of a teacher is becoming a process, time-limited to make him/her an effective classroom operative and little more' (Newbold, 1997 p2). Hill argues that the shift is towards 'de-theorized, de-intellectualized, technicist 'how-to' ITE courses' (Hill, 1994b p227), now constituting a 'curriculum for conformity' (Hill, 1997 p26). Recent research into school-based ITE has suggested that teaching models of this kind are inadequate, leaving students poorly prepared to tackle issues such as equal opportunities and special educational needs (Garner, 1996). It has been argued that the recommendations made by the Council for the Accreditation of Teacher Education (CATE) offer particular forms of behaviouristic and craft models of teacher education that 'adequately prepare teachers to become skilled clerks or bureaucrats' (Busher and Simmons, 1993 p14).

Others are even angrier. Gilroy analyses how central control of the ITE curriculum has been achieved, how membership of CATE has been used as a legitimising tool for political purposes, how the voice of the professional was marginalised out of existence in the 'consultation' process, and concludes that this constitutes no less than 'political rape' of ITE (Gilroy, 1992). CATE's successor, the Teacher Training Agency (TTA) has attracted escalating criticism for being a powerful and influential body on which there is no-one who represents the professional voice of the teaching profession, and is no more than another government quango (Baty, 1997).

Since the change of government the role of the TTA has already begun to shift, and the agenda may be moving towards encouraging further expeditions into school-based training. This is an economic exercise which seeks to reclaim monies top-sliced by universities and relocate them directly at the point of training: the school. It establishes further grounds for the closure of ITE departments (based on Ofsted results and the control of student numbers), thereby effectively removing some dissenting voices completely and muting others. My research suggests that these moves will not promote a better understanding of equality issues, nor serve the best interests of children like Assan and Wayne.

Equal opportunities has already been seriously eroded from the teaching education agenda. Evidence from senior members of the National Curriculum Council shows that pressure was exerted on them by Ministers to see multicultural education as a 'no-go area' (Tomlinson, 1996 p37). Crozier and Menter (1993) highlighted examples of how the issue has faded from DES consultation papers and circulars, culminating in total extinction in the consultation document on *The Reform of Initial Teacher Training* (DES, 1992a), the first to ignore the issue of equal opportunities completely. The Secretary of State's criteria in circular 14/93 (CATE, 1993a and 1993b) which followed, also made absolutely no reference to ethnic or cultural diversity. Whereas earlier publications gave credence to equal opportunities (for example DES, 1984, CATE, 1989 point 6.2), Circular 14/93 listed thirty three competences by which newly qualified teachers should be judged, none of which related in any way to ethnic diversity, class or gender issues. Nor did it mention any forms of disadvantage or inequality.

These omissions remove the issue of equal opportunities completely from the agenda of initial teacher education. Further, in relegating the subject of multicultural education to nothing more than a sub-issue within the non-issue of equal opportunities (which now does not even feature as a desirable criterion of newly qualified teachers' competence), there is little incentive for its inclusion on courses of initial teacher education:

> Recent upheavals in the state education system have adopted a de-racialised discourse that has all but obliterated race equality issues at the national policy level (Gillborn, 1996 p175).

Issues of social justice were afforded no place on the DfEE teacher training documentation of 1998. Without equality requirements at national policy level, how can teacher educators in the 'white high-lands' be convinced equality issues are of value? Primary classroom teachers and mentors will not suddenly grapple with the issue of social justice and incorporate it in an education programme for which they themselves have had little or no preparation.

In at the deep end

Consideration of the role of the mentor returns me to my data, and the alarmingly poor quality of provision offered to beginning teachers on both courses. There are problematic issues in the relationship between Laura and Annette, and we saw that Helen's Headteacher took the view 'that we are expected to more or less throw them in at the deep end'. For some students, relationships with their supervising teacher or mentor were professionally productive and personally rewarding. For others, they were characterised by less desirable features such as the systematic removal of any non-contact time, observational time or discussion/reflection time. One supervising teacher explained his understanding of this process in more detail:

Craig	When she came to me, I threw her in and she had a full teaching load. She did that for three weeks so she knows what it feels like. She survived. And it was survival.
Russell	And that was deliberate?
Craig	Yes. I mean I didn't sort of arrange this with her, I just wanted to put her into that situation because I (silence).
Russell	You were there to support her?
Craig	Yes, I was always there to support her, but the idea was (pause) I wanted her to feel that she could say 'I survived a full teaching load'. Now we have come back and I have taken two days off her a week, well she sort of gets a day off complete, but it is split up through the week, and I help her out in a lot more ways now and I am in the class a lot more now.
Russell	So was that your decision or was that the school's policy?
Craig	No, that was just mine ... we have not been told how to deal with a student. I have no (pause) I have just been given the bumpf and told to look after the student.

When I questioned this student in the last week of her school experience, the 'two days off a week' were yet to happen and she was close to tears when she told me:

> I felt that the work I was doing wasn't up to the quality it should be, either by myself or by the children really. I was *coping* more than anything else. After the first four weeks I spoke to Craig about it and he said 'I've kind of done it on purpose because now you know you can cope. You could go to a school tomorrow and you could be a teacher', but I said 'All I have proved is that I can cope and that's it' and he said 'OK, now I'll give you some time, some more school time to plan in more detail, keep up to date with your college work' and I said 'That's great' (pause) but as of yet that hasn't happened. I've taught all week bar one lesson and half an hour this morning. I'm feeling absolutely shattered...

Yet again, none of this frustration was fed back to the university supervisor at any stage for fear of showing some kind of weakness in school, or for not living up to the professional expectations being made of her. Those who recommend that schools should be the senior partner in the training relationship (Beardon *et al.*, 1992) need to be thinking about this reality. It is easy to say that these are isolated incidents and that more care could be taken over the selection of partner schools, but my data reveals that it has been possible for schools to respond to all legislation, curricular changes and inspections with a blatant manipulation of student placements. Even when such schools and tutors are hand-picked by the ITE institution (as in Helen's case) there can still be significant in-adequacies.

As schools begin to take on a more significant role in ITE and some university tutors feel justified in intervening less overtly when they make school visits, students can feel that the HEI is failing them. Some find little support from either the school or the HEI. About her tutor's support during the weeks she was left alone in the classroom, Laura said:

> (Tutor) was just in and out. He never saw me open a lesson and he never saw me close a lesson, if that gives you any idea of the level of support. It's so annoying because one dinnertime he just waltzed in, sat there you know, like this on the desk and then went before the lesson finished. I said 'Are you not going to give me some feedback?' and he said 'It was OK'. You know, what use is that to you?

Although other students also disclosed a dearth of professional support in schools, not all found the experience distressing.

Jessica, (a student on the university-based course) had been placed in a school which had staffing difficulties. The Head was about to undergo a medical operation which he knew would require long-term convalescence and the newly appointed Deputy had been informed that she was to cover in his absence. Jessica was due to start her school experience in the Deputy's class, in which ten children had been identified as having special needs. At the end of her school experience Jessica told me:

> I think my problem in the first three weeks was Claire (the Deputy Head). The old Headteacher was constantly dragging her out, and so I had her class right from day one and I couldn't see how she had treated special needs. So basically I have been the class teacher here ... from the second I take the class no one comes in and disturbs me. It's just me and the children, I love it. I've learnt so much more by being on my own (pause) because if I make a mistake nobody is there to watch over me so I can learn from my mistakes without people judging me. It has been so helpful.

Again no word about this was relayed back to the supervising tutor, of whom Jessica says their was no sign during six of the nine weeks' attachment. Recent investigations of perceptions of school-based ITE by the various participants is revealing. Studies focused on students' perceptions and reflections on the most influential aspects of their courses, have concluded that students see class-room teachers and university tutors in equally positive terms (Furlong, 1990, Williams, 1994). When I asked my sample group to identify and discuss their most influential figure over their course, their responses were evenly distributed between the school and the university, but all were tightly bound up in the personal relationships they had built with either their university tutors or school mentors. I was surprised but found it interesting that two of the sample cited me as the most influential person in their teacher education, despite my peripheral role. They told me that for them, I was the one person over the year who appeared to be genuinely interested in their views and progress, that I had given them opportunities to express their ideas and I had asked questions that resonated with their professional practice at later stages of their school experience.

Another study (Menter and Whitehead, 1995) showed that 83.8% of primary coordinators felt that the new school-based ITE requirements resulted in too much or even far too much workload and extra responsibility for schools, whereas 36.6% of HEI staff felt that it was 'about right'. The people most often asked to take on ITE responsibilities are found to be those who are already over-worked and highly stressed (Anderson, 1994 p24) – which might partly explain the poor deal that some students seemed to be getting. An NUT survey of teachers' views in 500 primary schools revealed serious concern about the lack of prior consultation, the lack of formal training and the significantly increased workload experienced by primary mentors (NUT, 1995). There seems to be a notable discrepancy in how the partnership between primary schools and HEIs is perceived, but my data suggests that this might be due to lack of communication between the key participants. In most cases, I found that this problem could have been resolved by the students, but as their top priority is to move through the process without any conflict, it is surely inappropriate to place the responsibility for the quality of the ITE partnership on to the participant who has least power and most at stake.

So we can see why Jessica felt that being left alone to learn alongside the children, with nobody to criticise her, had given her a golden opportunity. Although she found this school experience to be a particularly powerful on a personal level it can hardly have helped to develop her sense of professional-self, or to become the critically reflective teacher that she needs to be. In short, it had been all too easy to mislead the university's supervising tutor into believing that all was well, because it suited everyone concerned to keep him in the dark. It suited the Deputy because she could have on the job training for Headship, and it suited the Head because he did not have to find any money from the budget to finance supply work. It suited Jessica because she had nobody to criticise her, and she was able to leave the school with a final report that stated 'She has readily adopted our whole school approach and works closely with other members of staff ... This has been a highly successful teaching practice'. The university tutor understandably received 'all the right noises' from the school and was no doubt among the 36.6% who believed the partnership was working. The question that nobody asked was how well this suited the educational needs of the children? Remember also this was a class of children of whom ten had formally identified learning difficulties.

Other supervising teachers and mentors were quick to criticise the university's teacher educators, typically asserting that: 'they are not in tune with what's happening at all'. One mentor told me:

David That's the thing with (names the school-based university). They operated this twelve month course. They seem to have this idea that if you've got a degree you can teach. That's rubbish! Absolute rubbish! You can't do that in Primary at all.

Russell When I was training we had to spend time learning about child development, how children grow and how children learn ...

David But when you get into the classroom that doesn't mean anything. That doesn't help you. That doesn't help you teach at all. It's really ridiculous.

This mentor argued that it was only the classroom experience that mattered in the training. Although he maintained that there was more to teaching than simply having a first degree, the job was nothing to do with learning about child development and how children learn. In which case, it is highly unlikely that this mentor would be able to articulate the professional concerns outlined here.

It has been suggested that there are two constraints on a completely school-based ITE – the teachers' lack of time to work with students and the marginality of ITE to the central purpose of schools, which is educating children. The conclusion is that 'Trying to play two roles is often more disabling than facilitating' (Robinson and Heyes, 1996 p123) (see also Dart and Drake, 1993 p183). This sums up my own dilemmas as a classroom-based teacher-mentor and it highlights some of the problematic issues inherent in the shift to school-based ITE in primary schools, particularly regarding issues of equality and social justice.

Ill-defined roles of teacher-mentors

This is the point at which to bring in a story of my own. When I was asked to be a teacher-mentor I realised that it would affect my role as class teacher. Two beginning teachers were placed in my school, which had a staff consisting of the Head, myself as Deputy Head and five class teachers. The Head gave the staff several reasons for accepting the long-term placements. He had professional and personal relationships that he wanted to maintain with members of the university, he was keen to enhance the school's profile in the eyes of the parents and neighbouring primary schools and there was the vague possibility of extra money for the school. Most importantly, he told me that this would create space for myself as Deputy Head to tackle some of the curriculum statements and policies that needed to be overhauled pre-OFSTED, to start outlining formal job descriptions and to initiate some preliminary teacher appraisal which would mean spending time working in a supportive role alongside each of my colleagues. The class teacher who was allocated the other student was similarly briefed. Such selling of the mentor role was not uncommon, as I discovered when I interviewed other mentors. One told me:

> Certainly, I've suffered this time from being a kind of cheap source of supply. I have been everywhere from Reception/Year One to Year Six in the last five weeks. Which you can understand. Everybody is strapped for cash aren't they?

Another mentor observed that:

> I know of people who have been mentors and people have made complaints that they weren't very good mentors and they were still being asked to be mentors again, but some people may see this as a good opportunity to get staff in and write policies and it is open to abuse.

The presumption was that our roles as mentors would be unproblematic in terms of articulating and demonstrating the skills, knowledge and craft of primary teaching, and that once we had achieved this we would pass the children over to the students and begin to take on more directed management tasks. It was made clear that we were expected to establish this level of competence before Christmas, when the beginning teachers would be three months into their PGCE course and would have had only a few weeks in the school.

The reality proved to be somewhat different to the Head's expectations and it is obvious with hindsight why there were unresolved problems. The school had a reputation for providing powerful first hand experiences for children, and both the interior and exterior environments demonstrated this clearly. We had just completed our commitment to the AEMS project and the school reflected large-scale input from residential visits with a Bermudan sculptor, a Nigerian painter and an Indian dancer. Each teacher-mentor was expected to have regular input from the university, beginning with a full day's input at the university, which would end with a meeting with their students. Supply cover was paid for as part of this agreement but the Head insisted that he attend in our places so as to save the money paid by the university to use for other school priorities. He promised to pass on any relevant information. In reality, this meant that he passed on some paperwork and told us that we were not to call our two protégés 'students' but must always refer to them as 'associate teachers'.

Gillian was the kind of beginning teacher who found the whole experience of being in school extremely problematic, and it was several weeks before she even felt confident to communicate with the children in the class. Members of the university staff later explained that she had been placed with me because my contribution to the ethos of the school would help her to 'come out of her shell'. In the early stages my colleagues would invent notices and send them to me so that I could ask her to read them out at the end of the day, but she found even this level of communication intensely stressful and several times she refused. I had organised a field trip for my class to Manchester to attend a play and visit an art gallery, and even though the children tried to start conversations about this with Gillian, they met with silence and eventually stopped trying.

When I raised my initial concerns about Gillian I was told that perhaps I needed to slow the process down, in order to facilitate a more gradual induction into teaching. Over the coming months the vast majority of my time was spent in reassuring her, encouraging her to take a more active role in the classroom, helping her to piece together ideas for lessons, showing her how to manage resources, and gradually building up her confidence to the point where she was able to commit herself to the preparation, delivery and assessment of a lesson for most of the class.

I felt enormous professional pressure during the nine months Gillian was in my class, as this was the first time in my career that I felt I was not living up to the professional expectations held of me. I realised that I had no idea how to turn this student into a teacher at the pace demanded by the university. I was conscious that I was not getting the non-contact time the Head had predicted to generate new school policies and ideas. I could see that Gillian was not settling to the task of teaching, as both 'associate teachers' declared that they were not keen to teach once they had qualified because it was 'too much like hard work'. Worst of all, I knew just how damaging the whole process had been to the children and their learning. In addition, we knew that this course was a trial year in order to validate future school-based ITE, and we had been instructed by the university that none of the original twelve students was to fail the course.

This experience dovetails with the fact that the government's own pilot scheme for school-based training was declared a success even before it was completed (Blake, 1994 p55). As the end of the year approached, the Head, my teacher-mentor colleague and I all had grave doubts about Gillian's progress. She had begun to organise and deliver some schemes of work but clearly had a very long way to go before reaching the standards expected of a professional teacher. When the course was completed, my teacher-mentor colleague and I both felt exhausted. What was intended to be a year in which we would be able to consolidate our own practice and address some wider issues had turned into the most frustrating and professionally distressing year of our careers. Our experiences would seem to reflect those of other teacher mentors at the time, who featured in a report which established serious concerns about school-based training, and concluded that 'It is a tribute to the commitment of teachers that these school-administered programmes were able to take place at all, given the inadequate lead-in time' (Pyke, 1995b).

It was only after the course had ended – our concerns being persistently ignored – and the two beginning teachers had passed successfully, that I realised that not once had I discussed with Gillian any aspect of my work in multicultural education. Having been (presumably) the single most important person involved in her teacher education (being both her teacher-mentor and one of her university lecturers) and having demonstrated so much recent commitment to the subject of multicultural education, I found it both astonishing and depressing that I had never managed to raise this as an issue with Gillian. All my concerns and professional efforts had been to give her a set of baseline skills to transmit a given body of knowledge, the results of which bore no resemblance whatsoever to the teaching and learning ethos of the school. It makes an enormous difference when discussing the experiences of my sample group to know that I had first hand experience of this kind of educative process and consequently knew how easy it was for the dialogue process to disintegrate into a 'Blue Peter' model of training.

When research identifies where the professional dialogue between teachers and learners becomes problematic, some of these issues become visible in the ITE process. The difficulties that lie ahead with the political shift towards school-based ITE are more predictable in the light of these experiences. How can our beginning teachers experience high quality training if successful and experienced classroom teachers are expected to prepare the next generation of teachers while having their own practice undermined? How can they do so if they are expected to act as unlimited supply teachers so as to protect the school's budget, and if they are bundled into a position where the root philosophy underpinning successful practice is absent from a professional ITE dialogue so that they can achieve only a technical mode of teaching and training? The quality of new teacher graduates will not be enhanced if the teachers responsible for training them are forbidden (nine months earlier) from ever failing a student because it would not be in the university's economic interests. Our next generation of teachers are unlikely to achieve effective teaching and learning relationships with children if they are trained by 'professionals' who perceive children as 'thickos' and 'as thick as pig shit'. This data can be seen as revealing the inevitable by-product of an education system which has systematically refused to acknowledge the centrality of social justice, and which repeatedly dismisses the issues as irrelevant, university-based theory.

The TTA

We have seen how right wing think tanks such as the Adam Smith Institute, the Social Affairs Unit and the Centre for Policy Studies have influenced government policy, asserting that the curriculum was 'dominated by a mish-mash of equal opportunities and progressive ideology' (Blake, 1993 p15). In a speech to the North of England Education Conference the then Secretary of State for Education openly confirmed the Government's stance:

> The college-based parts of training must be fully relevant to classroom practice. The acid test must be whether or not the models they offer can actually be made to work effectively by the average teacher in the real classroom. That is the way to break the hold of the dogmas about teaching method and classroom organisation which are now being challenged not only by me but by very many other people (DES, 1992b para 21).

It is within this context that the establishment of the TTA should be considered. The TTA favours school-based initial teacher *training* and dismissive of the role of HEIs. Any lingering doubts were resolved when the TTA's Chief Executive proclaimed that 'Initial teacher training is not an academic subject and therefore (not) an intrinsic part of higher education' (quoted in Baty, 1997 p3). Having thus dismissed the educative role of the universities, 'consultation' documents (TTA, 1997) contained no reference whatsoever to multicultural education and demonstrated no commitment towards wider issues of social justice as part of a compulsory initial teacher education programme. This in spite of the CRE's accusation some nine months earlier that the Department for Education and Employment (DfEE) was being 'ostrich like' in its refusal to address race issues to do with underachievement and ethnic monitoring (Pyke, 1996 p1). When I contacted the TTA about these issues and asked for any documentation referring to multi-cultural education in ITE I was met with silence. Following my instincts, I said 'You haven't heard of multicultural education have you?'. This was the reply:

> No, I've not heard of multicultural education. I am not aware that it is a particular requirement of the National Curriculum. I can see why it may be more appropriate in multicultural areas or you might find it linked to things like education about drugs (TTA representative, 10.6.96).

This response may well not be the official TTA line on the issue, but it is extremely enlightening on several levels. Firstly, it devalues the subject instantly because it is not a 'particular requirement of the National Curriculum' and therefore not one which requires a stock answer. Secondly, it is presumed that it is not an appropriate issue for the 'white highlands'. Thirdly, and frighteningly, the concept of ethnic minorities and multiculturalism is unproblematically linked with drug abuse.

In 1998 the Chair of the CRE accused the TTA of 'sticking two fingers up' at issues of racial justice in education (Ghouri, 1998). The only response from the TTA's Director was a protest that they were making efforts to recruit more ethnic minority teachers. Not the same thing at all.

Similarly, when I requested information from the DFEE on any circulars relating to the issue, I received a letter which began:

> I have not found any circulars concerning multi-cultural education in primary schools. I hope that the attached press notice is of some interest/use, but please note that it is ten years old (Personal correspondence with DfEE 12.6.96).

Where next?
It cannot be expected that a change of government would bring about an immediate resolution to these issues. Nevertheless, party politics and ITE reform have now become part of the educational agenda for Headteachers (Rafferty and Dean, 1996 p1). School-based ITE is receiving all-party support, but the difference lies in the nature and quality of that relationship, and the specific role that universities will play. The Labour party have begun the process of

overhauling ITE, bringing the role of the university into clearer focus. *The Times Educational Supplement* reported that:

> All teacher training would take place in partnerships between schools and universities, with a stronger role for the universities both in initial training and professional development. Labour envisages that all schools would eventually be involved (Gardiner, 1996b p2).

If there is to be a stronger role for HEIs within the university/ school partnership, wider issues need resolution before one can begin to discuss upgrading issues of social justice. Removing budgets originally located in the hands of LEAs specifically for financing higher degrees by practitioners has meant that not only are there fewer teachers who follow traditional M.Ed or MA (Ed) programmes, but that INSET now typically consists of shorter courses reflecting the need to meet National Curriculum directives, to advance the role of the curriculum coordinator to meet OFSTED needs and generally to cover the changing nature of assessment and education management post ERA (Coffey, 1992 p111). In the past the key to the development of multicultural issues in rural primary schools was found to be the appointment of committed LEA advisors (Pearse, 1989 p280), but since this was recommended the local advisory service has been similarly depleted.

New legislation could be interpreted as constructing a profession where theory and reflection become marginalised in the drive towards a technicist model of competence based teaching. Creating a working relationship between schools and universities will not guarantee that those relationships work well. Designers of school-based PGCE courses for primary teachers have listed the problems they found in assigning mentors to students, in working towards providing equity of experience, and in securing enough suitably qualified schools who were prepared to take on the extra training responsibilities (Whitehead *et al.*, 1994). Moreover, the Modes of Teacher Education (MOTE) Project identifies the 'constant theme' (of) 'the fragility of the system as a whole' (Whiting *et al*, 1996 p78). There are also wider fundamental issues related to the structure and formal requirements of the National Curriculum, to the allocation and prioritisation of INSET budgets and the perennial issue of non-contact time in primary schools, all of which need to be addressed simultaneously if there is to be a real community of learners in which beginning teachers can find a place.

At the start of my study, I would not have imagined that beginning teachers such as Laura would have been placed in professional situations where their supervising teachers were able to exert such a negative influence on their education. Nor would I have expected to see such meagre provision as Jessica received being counted as main school experience. The ITE provided for all my sample students raises fundamental questions about the efficacy of the school-based model. Helen's story, Kim's story and Laura's story all indicate clear needs to raise issues of social justice during their training. It becomes all the more obvious through the telling of these stories that whilst the changing nature of ITE holds all kinds of pitfalls, the space for dealing with issues of social justice becomes further restricted, and issues of race in the 'white highlands' constitute an increasingly disembodied debate. If issues of race can be systematically disregarded by schools and universities during the current ITE process, they could become equally irrelevant in new models. No policy directives place social justice on the agenda of educational provision for children.

For most of my sample, race was never an issue. Either they saw no ethnic minority children in their schools at all, or – as the next chapter relates – ethnic minority children were present in the classroom but were in some way conceptually erased from the professional perceptions of these beginning teachers. These exclusively white students taught by their exclusively white lecturers, working with exclusively white teachers in predominantly white schools and teaching a white curriculum unsurprisingly thought it strange that I should want to talk about issues of ethnicity. It is precisely the disappearances, omissions and silences that became the substantive matter of my research. The three stories told so far have been selected as exceptional. These are the cases where race was an issue, where it *was* possible to peek beneath the surface sheen of unproblematic ITE and see causes for concern. At best, the strategies employed by these students to deal with issues such as race were misguided. At worst they constituted a distinct curriculum of which confirming prevailing racism was a taught element.

Chapter 6

Rachel's Story

race: training and learning

The three stories told so far build a picture of the ways in which race was experienced by the beginning teachers while they were training in schools. This fourth and final story looks more closely at the role of the two universities to see if their input helped the students towards some greater understanding of issues of social justice.

From the onset, the course documentation from the two institutions did little to suggest the notion that multicultural education would be an important part of the course. There was no mention at all of equal opportunities or multicultural input on the timetable for the year on the university-based course, although the handbook stated that:

> Ethnicity and gender provide useful dimensions from which to view the learning/teaching process together with consideration of children with special educational needs.

Leaving aside the implied passivity, it is worrying that ethnicity is so directly linked with special educational needs. A beginning teacher could immediately equate ethnicity issues with behavioural and/or learning difficulties. Documentation from the school-based university course made reference to a 'bilingual pupils' session and an 'RE/multicultural' session at the end of the course, and one stated aim of the course was to develop 'an awareness of individual differences among pupils, including social, psychological, developmental and cultural dimensions'.

The university-based course provided a half day trip to a local Islamic centre and a Sikh temple. The school-based course offered an equal opportunities programme of four half days spread over the year, to include visits to a mosque and a synagogue. The co-ordinator for this element of the RE course explained that this would consist of an introductory half day on equal opportunities, half a day on multicultural education, half a day on English as a second language and half a day 'looking at other cultures', all in preparation for their full day's visit to a Mosque and a Synagogue in Manchester. Unfortunately these visits were cancelled because the lecturer fell ill.

Although I was given permission to attend all the stated elements on each course I had a problem when the university-based course's field trip and the school-based course's initial equal opportunities lecture were scheduled for the same morning. While I was still deciding which one to attend, I was informed that the school-based course's equal opportunities lecturer had been taken ill, but that the session would still go ahead, led by two other course tutors. Although I was assured that I could still witness the session, I was given the distinct impression that the course leader was uncomfortable about it, so I chose to attend the university-based course's field trip in the morning, then speak informally to the students on the school-based course about their equal opportunities session in the afternoon, when I was scheduled to be leading them in a three hour art session.

Rachel was a beginning teacher on the school-based course, with a social background similar to Kim's. She came from a family of three generations of teachers and had attended an all girls secondary school. She was articulate about her views on education and, like Kim, had the admirable aim of establishing a class of 'independent learners'. When I was trawling through the incoming students on the course and during the initial interviews, Rachel was the only one to talk about her interest in education in terms of quality, truth, respect, beauty, patience and the creativity of children. I recalled how I was shaped by just these educational ideals during the year's input I received as a newly qualified teacher, but as a course leader on LEA residential courses for newly qualified teachers, I could see how provision and support for this philosophy had diminished over the years. I knew that Rachel's views were not shared by others in her group and that the social dynamics of her peers had restricted her opportunities to speak further on these issues. During the initial group interviews I doubted whether she would have the opportunity to explore these ideas further in school, as Rachel's mentor told me:

> As far as I'm concerned, when they are post-grads, they have done all the writing and the academic bit, so what now they need to do is the skills of teaching. I mean the essays about whatever it is they write about, to me are a bit irrelevant, because obviously they are academics to have got onto the course.

Although Rachel had agreed to be part of my sample group, and despite the interest I had in her ideas, I had not selected her as one of my four case studies. Originally, I chose Michelle, a mature student who expressed deep concerns early in the course about her suitability for the job of teaching, as she felt she was being asked to surrender her working class identity in order to achieve some perceived middle class status as a teacher. She explained that she was being labelled by her neighbours as the 'stuck-up cow who's getting above herself' and worried that her husband's tattoos would be a problem if she ever had to socialise with fellow teachers. I would have liked more time working with Michelle, especially as she was criticised in school by her university tutor for her regional accent – the same regional accent as the children and the staff in the school where she was working, and which she interpreted as 'I was told I can't *speak*, because I'm *common*'.

I met Michelle as arranged, before I took her group for their art session in the afternoon. She arrived late from the morning's equal opportunities tutorial and explained that she needed to go into her partner school, and that although she was happy to remain as part of the wider sample group, she suspected she would find it difficult to offer the extra time I had said I needed for my case studies. I reluctantly accepted her decision.

Repercussions from one-off lectures

Preparing to take the afternoon session with the group, I met Jane, one of the two lecturers who had led the equal opportunities session. She told me that the morning had begun with a video for the whole group, followed by discussion in two groups. One of the students in her group, whom she did not name, had said 'some outrageously racist things', and Jane wanted to talk about the incident in more detail later. When everyone left after my session, I noticed that Rachel was still in the room. She was very subdued and I was aware that she had been quiet throughout the afternoon. I still had the tape recorder I had intended to use with Michelle, and so I asked Rachel if she wanted to talk. She agreed and we moved into a colleague's room where I set up the tape recorder. Rachel immediately burst into tears. I offered to switch off the tape but she assured me that she did not mind being recorded. The resulting conversation convinced me that she would be the ideal replacement case study.

Rachel said that the morning's equal opportunities session had deteriorated into what she felt was a personal attack, as she had been singled out by Jane for her racist views. She related how she had offered suggestions in open discussion that were seized upon by the tutor:

> Things like having Asian or black children in a class. Jane said that she felt ashamed when she went into one class because it was a new Year Three class and she went into the staffroom afterwards, they said to her 'Oh, how many Asian children have you got in your class?' and she said she didn't know. She hadn't noticed. I think that's *wonderful*. I think that is the way we *should* be. They had all been treated as children, every individual need had been catered for and she hadn't bothered to count who was white and who was brown and (pause) she was ashamed of that and thought that was wrong. She felt she should have noticed how many children there were. I disagreed.

She offered a few further examples from the morning's debate but it later came to light that her real concern had stemmed from something else, but that she felt too embarrassed to discuss it with me. I began to piece together the details over subsequent interviews with Rachel, and when I later spoke about the session to Jane, she told me:

We had had a general discussion about all the things that had cropped up in terms of stereotypes and gender roles as well as race (pause). It was challenging. It was challenging me because it was quite early on. They were also challenging each other across the table. It was related to what they had seen and just heard, but also to what went on in their own schools. At one point, quite late on, we had done perhaps three quarters of an hour so we were well into it, Rachel said (pause) she was sitting on my immediate left, so I couldn't actually see her face, but she said 'Well I don't see, Jane, why we can't push forward coloured children in terms of PE and sports and music, because everybody knows they are good at those things. Why do we deny it?' and several people made responses to her and I just said 'Can you say that about a whole group of people? Is every black person good at PE and good at music?' and she said 'Well, yes, generally they are'.

Rachel discussed this incident during two of her later interviews, and she remembered it quite differently:

It was a tutor group session where we were talking about multicultural issues and racism and stereotypes and (pause) I said something. As a statement it was misguided. I said something about black people being better dancers but that isn't what I meant. It was more a cultural impression but I didn't have a chance to qualify it... I phrased it wrongly at the time. You know, when you are thinking and stuff just comes out all at once and it is only when you take a step back that you can explain exactly what you mean, but Jane picked up on this and made me feel stupid. She made me feel really ignorant and racist really. And I think that is something that (pause) ignorant yes, in some respects, but never racist. Racism and multicultural issues are something I get very upset about, when I see inequality or (pause) bigoted behaviour anywhere, it is something I feel very strongly about, but yes, I was made to feel like a racist really and I didn't have a chance to defend myself. I think I tried once and everyone else was going (*demonstrates hiding her eyes in embarrassment*) putting their head in their hands. So I just shut up in the end.

Jane's session created a new agenda for equal opportunities on the course. Every one of my school-based sample group mentioned this incident at some point in their interviews. Some had been in Rachel's group and had witnessed it directly, others were keen to discuss it even though they had been in the parallel tutorial group and had only heard about it afterwards. Listening to them at the time and re-reading the transcripts at later stages, I can see just how influential this incident had been. Among the comments made in the round of interviews following this session, were:

> Jane really slagged people down...It was almost as though it was 'If you are not going to agree with me then I am not going to listen to it'.

> It went too far...It was just so dogmatic, I can't quite fathom it...it's like when you say something, innocently, and they bite, they snap back at you and there is something going on in their heads that makes you stand back and say 'Wayyy, what's going on here?'

> Russell   What do you remember about the equal opportunities day?

> Michelle   Heated debate. Jane arguing with Rachel. (laughs) ... she attacked her ... it was frightening.

> I remember her (Jane) going really blotchy and her blood pressure going up, I don't know what it was. I just felt like 'What's going on?' but I didn't say very much.

The response to 'not say very much' was understandably common, as the group felt individually threatened. But there was a greater consequence to follow. The second of the four sessions was scheduled to be the one on 'multiculturalism', and this was to be taught solely by Jane. In reality, this also turned out to be the last of the sessions, as she unexpectedly left the course. The format for this session was to be a full afternoon's programme of lectures and videos, followed by workshops centred around prepared newspaper clippings, and this was to be attended by Rachel along with my entire sample group as part of a whole class input. I was present for the whole session, still unaware (at that time) of the depth of feeling among many of the students towards Jane, and hence, for some of them, towards the issue of multicultural education itself. I made detailed field notes about the proceedings and interviewed Jane shortly afterwards. It was only during my next round of interviews that I began to understand more fully the dynamics of the afternoon.

I noted that the session ran for two hours and forty five minutes without a break and that it was attended by twenty nine of the remaining thirty one course members. Jane set a clear agenda for the afternoon and opened the proceedings with statements such as:

> I don't want to hear 'this isn't important because we haven't got any coloured (sic) children in our school', I'm going to say it is more important in schools where the children don't see any coloured children or children from other cultures ... You probably feel that you are not racist, but I am and you are.

She also acknowledged some discomfort following the earlier session, stating:

> It is a sensitive issue but we do need to have our thoughts and beliefs challenged. After the video we will open it up for discussion. I don't want World War Three but I do want us to air our prejudices and ignorances.

By the start of the video no student had said a word. The video itself drew on newsreel footage highlighting condescending narratives, stereotyped images of black people used in advertising and sweeping racial generalisations made in the media. After some discussions about Jane's personal experiences of name-calling, some newspaper clippings about racial incidents were distributed for group discussion and feedback. This activity was misunderstood by some of the groups, who wandered off into debates about whether punks and skinheads were 'asking for trouble with the police', and whether age was an issue as younger drivers were 'more likely to be stopped by the police'. Jane sensitively steered the conversations back on task as each group reported back their findings.

Rachel was the spokesperson for her group, giving an appraisal of an article about crime statistics and links with ethnic minorities. Some dispute of these statistics followed and Rachel reformulated her group's initial response in favour of a more sensitive reading, which Jane openly acknowledged and praised. My field notes record how I felt that the session had a variety of interesting focal points, raised some valid issues and was handled sensitively by the lecturer. It was difficult however, to overlook the students' lack of response to her input, which was surprising considering that there was a close knit group of twenty nine students in a small room. When I later asked Jane who she thought had contributed most, she named six students, all coincidentally amongst my sample group of ten. This seemed to confirm my suspicion that a large part of my initial decision about the sample group had rested on their willingness to discuss ideas in an open forum.

It was clear from the data collected over the following weeks that there had been a shared sub-text to Jane's multicultural session that I had not identified at the time. Even the most positive response I received acknowledged that it had been a strange experience:

James	It was very interesting. I liked it. She raised some issues which needed to be confronted. I was a bit aware of the fact that not many people were really saying much.
Russell	Did you think that maybe people were threatened by it?
James	That was what I wanted. I wanted somebody to be threatened by it, to actually respond to it but they didn't. They just sat there and I thought 'Well is this (pause) is everybody keeping quiet because we know all this stuff and we don't need this kind of lecture, or is it because they don't want to say something because they'll be in the minority?'. It was really interesting because there was nothing. It went really silent, didn't it? Did you feel it?

When I later raised the issue (separately) with the beginning teachers, some of them seemed to recall the silence more readily than anything that was said:

Russell	Do you remember the equal opps day at the university?
Laura	(silence)
Russell	The day that Jane ran?
Laura	Err, (laughs) (pause). Yes I do, vaguely (laughs).
Beth	I can't remember what we did, which must tell us something. Maybe it was just that I was particularly tired that day.
Michelle	I'm lost as to what we did, so it couldn't have made that much of an impression. I remember we looked at some newspaper clippings but (pause) if it had stood out (pause) do you know what I mean. If it had meant that much.

Several of the others present, however, felt considerable resentment about the session that had little or nothing to do with the
issue but was directed at the lecturer:

> Oh, well (pause) she has bees in her bonnet about things doesn't she?
> She only wants to hear what she wants to hear...We had to look at
> newspaper clippings and we had to say what we thought was wrong
> about them, and it was almost like 'God, if you couldn't spot what was
> wrong, you know...you're not spot on are you?'.

Grace	It could have been done better. It didn't all go in.
Russell	You don't really remember it then?
Grace	I think that it was the lecturer to be honest. To be perfectly honest.

> For a situation where we are talking about taking on board other
> people's ideas, ways of life and that, I think Jane is very single tracked, you
> know.

The following exchange seems to typify the depth of feeling about
the day:

Russell	How did you think the equal opps day went with Jane?
Donna	(silence) Remind me.
Russell	There was a video and newspaper clippings.
Donna	What do you want me to say?
Russell	I don't know.
Donna	Who is hearing this?
Russell	You and I. Nothing will ever be reported in your name outside of this room. You will never be able to be identified by anything you ever say to me.
Donna	(silence)
Russell	I solemnly swear (laughs). Tell me what you thought.
Donna	I thought it was a complete waste of time. Because Jane looks for racism when it just isn't there. Then it gets to the point where people don't answer because unless it is what Jane wants to hear you are wrong (pause) I just got to the

point where I thought 'Well what is the point?'. I can't quite understand why she is so hot on equal opportunities and racism because everybody just sits there and nobody speaks because they get a sense of 'It's my opinion and that's all that counts'. Well you asked me!

Jane acknowledged that there was a strange atmosphere during the session but presumed that this was because she was dealing with a contentious issue and that the students did not feel comfortable about exposing their own prejudices. Afterwards, she explained that Rachel's contribution was:

> The most important point of the whole session ... I've never seen the change so marked as the way my perception of Rachel on that day and my perception of Rachel on Monday ... it changed immeasurably. For me ... I just went away and I said 'If nothing else that was really, really important'.

Considering that the multicultural session had been a negative experience for so many students, and that the reason for this stemmed directly from the way that Rachel had been handled in the earlier tutorial group, this summation from Jane is intriguing. Jane refers not to any change in Rachel between the two sessions, but the change in *her own perception* of Rachel. In retrospect and given the advantage of hindsight, it could be argued that the 'immeasurable change' that was 'really, really important' was not about Rachel making an ideological shift on race issues but more about her recognition that perhaps her ideas had been misjudged. At the original tutorial meeting Jane understandably wanted to challenge what she perceived to be racist views held by a student, and she had recognised that the experience had been painful. She told me that:

> I could see she was obviously upset. You could see also in her face and in the way she puts things that they come from home and the worrying thing is that both her parents are teachers. She hadn't actually thought about them, it hadn't been an issue. I knew she was upset, I knew it was hard but it had to be because she was so far down the line. What I generally find with the students is that they pretend...

However, Jane shows a sense of confusion and doubt in her assessment of the change in Rachel's view, because she goes on to develop her suspicions of pretence:

Maybe what she was doing was (pause) even if at this stage she didn't believe what she actually said, at least she felt that 'At least I'm going to be politically correct, and this is what I should be saying', so she is thinking about it.

Perhaps Jane is right, and Rachel had merely learnt to give answers that are 'politically correct', but even if this were true, the way this was achieved and its effect on the remaining students has serious implications. Rachel's original statement was, by her own admission 'ignorant' and 'misguided', but Jane's confrontational challenge did not allow her to explore why her ideas were perceived as racist and she was not allowed to retract her statement nor to qualify what she was trying to articulate. She was, however, afforded this space at the later multicultural session and this may be why Jane changed her opinion of her. If there was indeed a 'dramatic change' in Rachel as suggested by Jane, it was less likely a result of the formal multicultural input and more to do with the fact that she had been allowed to explore her own ignorances and to articulate the naiveté she recognised in herself. Unfortunately, by this time the subtext of the session was out of Jane's control. The withdrawals and silences of the afternoon were the result of a mixture of fear about offering suggestions lest they too earned public humiliation and, secondly, a deliberate intention to refrain from active participation out of resentment over Jane's earlier treatment of Rachel.

Resistance to 'political correctness'

The issue of the 'politically correct' answer came to assume importance during the equal opportunities sessions at both universities. Jane's experience of students who 'pretend' towards some form of 'political correctness' resonated deeply during the equal opportunities session at the end of the university-based course some six months later. The structure of this session was more formal and lecturer-led than at the school-based course, but many of the issues were raised in a similar way, the lecturer weaving in elements of her own considerable personal experience with documentary evidence and video footage. The main organisational difference was that this session relied on open contributions to a tutor-led discussion whereas the school-based session leant more heavily towards work-shops and smaller group discussions.

There were some initial doubts expressed by both the tutor and the university-based students about the timing of the session. One student said: 'it seems a farce to have the (multicultural) session now. We are all so unmotivated and so bored'. It was noticeable that this same concern was expressed by the course leader, who described the period as 'usually a vacuum', elaborating that multi-cultural education was going to be covered at this time alongside issues such as governors, bullying and OFSTED in order, he said, 'to fill the gap'. The student responses to the afternoon, however, ranged from 'It was brilliant' and 'It was a really good lecture' to 'I wasn't impressed. I found it patronising, I'm afraid' and 'It just seemed pretty pointless'. Despite the fact that the lecturer had, on several occasions, deliberately used her own life experiences as a route into dealing with equal opportunity issues, one student com-mented:

> It was just the history. I knew everything about the Education Reform Acts and that's all it was. It was the history. It would have been better if we had talked about what it meant to us and I had a lot of feelings about how do we deal with it? There were no questions at the end, she didn't answer anything, she just wanted our views and she should have sug-gested 'perhaps if you do this ...'

Andy and John were two of the men on the university-based course who did not respond to my initial appeal for participants in the study, and consequently were not part of my sample group. They made a point at the start of the session that several students later told me they found particularly interesting but felt had been over-looked, and they thought that it would have been a better experience for the group if they had been allowed to follow it up. The men had suggested that if the session was about equal oppor-tunities it ought to address the issue of regionalism and regional accents, as this had been a negative experience for several students in their schools. Just as Jane had perceived the discussions about punks and skinheads as marginal to the subject at hand and steered the proceedings back towards her own agenda, the university-based lecturer felt obliged to do likewise, gently explaining to the students at the time and later to me in interview that:

> Yes, there is Nationalism as an issue, there are issues about which we can feel very uptight and angry because they affect our lives, but they are not to the same degree as somebody who is visibly very different and cannot change that in any way, like you can get rid of your accent if you wish to, etc. you don't have to tell people that you are gay if you don't want to ... there isn't really any point in going down the road of saying 'But *my* issue is more important than *your* issue, and *my* disability is more important than *yours*' or 'Being a Jew you deserve more sympathy than being black', because you get into this sort of hierarchy of oppression and it doesn't do you any good.

This however, was perceived by several of the students as the lecturer 'ducking the issue'. Typical comments were:

> It would have been nice if that could have gone on all day, because then we could have developed that argument that Andy brought up from the early years. We could have carried on all day about that.

> When the questions started to be asked by Andy and John, I think if she had left it going and carried on from there it could have been excellent

> It is not as clear cut as she wanted to make it ... quite a few of us actually, when we came out we said we were very angry about that because it was just equally offensive. I mean I am from Liverpool and ... when I was living in Lancashire I came across what I would describe as racism.

For several of the students I interviewed their sense of having had no chance to discuss the regionalism issue was the overriding memory of the equal opportunities session. Their irritation seemed to me to be because none of them was black, none was disabled, none had really perceived any gender issues in school and here was a 'real' issue that had directly affected their sense of equal opportunities and they had not been allowed to discuss it. When I later presented some of these findings to a group of exclusively white final year B.Ed students at another institution of ITE, in Wales, this issue again rose as the overriding subject for debate. Starting points for the beginning teachers in Wales ranged from 'I feel threatened by these Pakis swamping the country' and 'If a white woman and a Paki woman went for a job in the same school and the Paki woman got it, then that's racism', to one student's argument that: 'What the English have done to the Welsh is no different to what Hitler did to the Jews'.

Kim was present at the university-based equal opportunities session and told me:

> It was interesting. It was very interesting, a lot of stuff you did think 'Oh yes, I ought to think about that'. But I am always wary of these things though and taking them too far.

Whereas I felt the session had focused quite clearly on multiculturalism, Kim felt that it had had little to do with multicultural issues:

> It was more to do with gender. I mean I suppose it is because in Midshire for instance, there isn't that much multicultural ... it's just not that far, I mean it is just a question of ... if you are going to be in that position you need to find out, you know, you need to research it a bit and read up about it so that you are not going to put your foot in it at all.

Jane's experience on the school-based course of 'pretence' and 'giving the tutor what they wanted to hear' also surfaced among several of my sample group and my field notes recall how surprised I was when Kim gave a perfectly 'politically correct' answer to one of the lecturer's direct questions, as by then I was well aware of her open hostility towards such issues. She noticed this irony when I pointed it out and later explained that 'giving the tutor what they wanted' was part of an ongoing 'game' of achieving the qualification:

> It is ridiculous, you just can't do it. What you end up doing (pause) don't tell anyone, what you end up doing is just making up half the things ... the children's work, the things that children are supposed to have said for assignments on the first practice. I just made them all up because (pause) everyone did because you can't (pause) you can't keep it all in your head.

This kind of approach to equal opportunities sessions is not uncommon. Kate Myers invented the term 'Equiphobia' to describe 'an irrational hatred of anything to do with equal opportunities' (cited in Siraj-Blatchford and Troyna, 1993 p223). A professor working in another predominantly white ITE institution found her beginning teachers displayed similarly dubious responses to multicultural issues and several of her findings resonate closely with mine (Ahlquist, 1992). She suggested that these students were performance oriented and felt uncomfortable addressing 'ambiguous' issues which offered no simple solutions and that several felt that racism and sexism no longer existed and that they had 'learned to distrust the use of such terms because all too often they are used as clubs to make them feel guilty' (Ahlquist, 1992 p97). The only study I located which claimed that beginning teachers were likely to enter the profession 'with a humanistic drive to view marginalized students positively' (Hlebowitsh and Tellez, 1993 p41) worked with a sample group of students of which 25% were non-white. This is surely going to yield very different results to work carried out in all-white institutions.

I was to discover that other 'games' were taking place in Kim's multicultural education lecture that suggested a more negative scenario. Sara, one of my four case studies, was another student who made regular and vociferous objections during our interviews to anything that she perceived to be remotely 'politically correct'. Her most sustained discussion on the subject was a bitter attack:

> I think there is a great deal of (pause) and I hate this word, 'right-on-ness' and I think that some people are too 'right-on' for their own good. They forget that they are dealing with people, and say 'Oh you can't do that because such-a-body says this and you're creating a social stigma'. I'm afraid that's crap! It makes me very angry because they seem to be so tunnelled in their vision that you've got to do this, this, this and this, but you haven't! These are people, not a category. It makes me very angry. I find this political correctness extremely misplaced and I have to say that I question somebody's morals who is that politically correct.

Sara told me that she and her friend had been challenging each other during the equal opportunities session to see which of them could give the 'politically correct' answer that elicited the most praise from the lecturer. Sara's actions were completely independent of Kim's, who (by her own, separate admission) was playing much the same 'game'. Sara went on to elaborate:

Sara   It was all very (pause) it was interesting and it was well prepared but I felt it was more like watching a lecturer.

Russell	Did you think it was challenging?
Sara	Not in any way, no. I mean that definition I gave her. That was the one she wanted.
Russell	Yes! I was amazed. After everything you had said to me.
Sara	And you know I don't like PC lines.
Russell	Yes.
Sara	And it is not because I am racist.
Russell	No, I know.
Sara	I don't see that people should be judged because of their colour, their sex, their class or anything because they are people first and foremost. They are human beings and you have the right to be treated as such so as far as I am concerned you should just see everyone as an individual and you should have the common decency to treat them as such, and so when she said 'we all like to think of ourselves as 'right on' (pause)'. I thought 'Hmmm' (laughs).
Russell	I couldn't help but watch you at that point.
Sara	(laughs).
Russell	So that day sums up why you don't like PC?
Sara	Yes. It was very tiresome (laughs) I'm sorry… I knew exactly what she was going to say. I could have done the lecture. I know it was very cynical, what I did, but (pause) that *is* what she wanted. It's *true* actually, that is what I think about racism and sexism but…
Russell	You seemed to say what she wanted.
Sara	It was *exactly* what she wanted. I'm sorry. I'm just being a horribly cynical person (pause) I suppose I tend to think I don't need PC because I don't have a problem with it, it is not an issue for me.

Just as Kim's university tutor had been so complimentary about her suitability as a teacher at the end of the year, so Sara's tutor enthused about her, saying:

> She is a very good teacher. She developed a very good relationship with the children she had. In fact it was very hard to fault her ... her relationships with the children were fine and with the staff it was super.

When I discussed them with her later in a formal interview the equal opportunities lecturer was not delighted about these 'games', but she said that this was not new in her experience with equal opportunities teaching. The one issue that became difficult for the lecturer to deal with was the students' resistance to 'political correctness'. Both university lecturers had tried to make the point in the equal opportunities sessions that 'we are all at different points along the politically correct continuum', but she found it difficult to understand that at least three of my sample had openly removed themselves from that continuum and had not only resisted any attempt to deal with the agenda, but had deliberately and actively set out to undermine it.

So I witnessed two equal opportunities sessions in different universities, sitting at the back of the room, taking notes, tape-recording relevant sessions, collecting and examining the handouts, and concluded that both were well prepared, well resourced and delivered in different but thought-provoking and entirely appropriate ways. In conversation with the students over the following weeks, however, I began to recognise the impotence of these conventional data gathering methods. This particular procedure – by far the most detached aspect of my entire data collection process – left me in no doubt about the dangers of presuming that it is possible to achieve a perfect 'God's eye' view of events. It was only the sustained relationships I had established with the students that had facilitated a sense of trust between us and elicited the crucial data. No amount of observation or document analysis would have yielded this, and I suspect that the only way to study a sensitive issue such as race is to establish similar long-term relationships with individuals and institutions.

I am equally certain that I was only able to collect this data because of my own ethnicity. Had I been black I would have generated very different transcription data even if I had asked exactly the same questions of exactly the same people. The whole business left me with the impression that I could access this information only because I am a white male primary teacher. I am reminded that on my first day of my Deputy Headship I was met by another member of staff who told me a joke about a 'nigger with a big dick'. In much the same way as this member of staff would not have told the same joke to a new black member of staff, much of what was told to me in interviews held the same unspoken presumption of shared belief.

At the end of the PGCE year, I had to accept that issues of social justice were not going to be a large part of the professional motivation in the generation of new teachers I had studied. Their universities would no doubt claim that on paper, as part of their teaching schedule, the students had formally covered multicultural education. My data however, indicated that although most students were physically present at the sessions, there were dynamics at work that ensured that the objectives of the lectures and workshops were never going to be met. The input from the universities was not entirely successful, but even more significant is the lack of input – or negative models – demonstrated by schools. In Kim's story, one teacher said:

> It's the job of the college. They've got enough staff, it's their job. Let's be honest here, who's getting their training done on the cheap? It's their job. I have never dealt with things like multicultural education with a student. It's not really an issue here anyway but it's the college who should be doing it.

Nothing in my data suggests that issues of social justice are going to be better handled in the shift towards school-based ITE. Indeed, if the schools believe it is the job of the university, and the universities can only expect further timetable restrictions, issues such as multicultural education are inevitably going to shrink towards vanishing point in teacher education.

How the partners view one another

It is important to understand how each side in the school/ university partnership perceives the needs and strengths of the other and how issues such as multicultural education might fit in this relationship. Several concerns were raised by university staff about the very nature of school-based ITE and the suitability of certain schools for the task. A particular concern was the lack of subject specialism and expertise of some primary schools. Some schools had begun to form cluster groups to pool subject specialism resources and others had made more use of subject advisors to meet identified curriculum weaknesses, but not all of the university primary subject lecturers were satisfied. It was presumed that subjects such as English, maths and science would be covered relatively well, but that subjects such as design and technology, art and information technology might well be taught by non-subject specialists and taken on as subsidiary areas of responsibility. It was suggested that not only would these teachers be poorly prepared conceptually to teach their pupils, but that their lack of subject knowledge would then be transferred to school-based students by those non-specialists, who would receive only piecemeal models of provision. One experienced lecturer made this clear:

> My greatest fear about school-based training is that in a subject like design and technology which is relatively new in National Curriculum terms certainly, very few schools had experienced it prior to National Curriculum, that there are not sufficient people who are experienced out in schools because...well it is a specialised subject. Unless you have had some formalised training you are unlikely to be able to offer good practice in the school. Therefore, whatever models trainee teachers see will be based on people who have not got the experience in the subject. My feeling is that a lot of it will be content led activities where the pupils make very similar or identical outcomes which people feel is addressing the content side of the National Curriculum but in fact it is not good practice in design and technology because the pupils are not being involved in the designing, the decision making, all the key issues of trial and error and learning through mistakes and so on.

Another lecturer put it even more forcefully:

> I think it is absolute bollocks. I really do. The anomaly is the government is saying to us (pause) well the *Daily Mail* would have us believe that all teachers are crap and yet the government wants us, well wants the teachers who are crap, to train the new generation of teachers and it is fucking bollocks, it really is.

Rachel's mentor, saw the university's formal requirements as an imposition and an irrelevant intrusion on the job of teacher training bears this out, and much work must be done on the quality of the school/university partnership before teachers acknowledge the relevance of 'theory' to the course. The views expressed by Rachel's mentor were not untypical of other mentors on the school-based course. Another told me:

> They do need to spend more time in schools as long as the university sends them along with a bit more of an open mind as opposed to all the theoretical books and ideas that they push them into.

Other research has suggested that some PGCE mentors believe that 'simply by dint of their greater expertise, they must be providing an effective service to initial teacher trainees' (Kerry and Farrow, 1996 p107), so are wary of any academic rigour expected of their students which might hinder the 'real' job of classroom teaching. Add to this the evidence to suggest that some beginning primary teachers, as recent pupils themselves, have demonstrated a tendency to see the pedagogical process as merely teaching and have little understanding of the factors affecting the learning process with young children (Edwards, 1996b p5), and it is clear that this misconception could be reinforced by mentors who wish to criticise the role of the university.

More naively, there seemed to be a presumption among beginning teachers and their mentors that the longer they spent in school the higher the quality of the beginning teacher's experiences. When I probed the reasons for this, I received answers like these:

> It's good for the school because ... you've got somebody who is treated like another member of staff and it's like another pair of hands (Mentor on school-based PGCE course).

> They can't take their feet off the pedal after five or six weeks (Head-teacher on university-based PGCE course).

> I don't think universities prepare you to teach...you need to be in the classroom. There's nothing better than learning in the classroom (Supervising teacher on university-based PGCE course).

> They are here when the photographer comes. They are here at Christmas when someone throws a wobbler, they are here when they are all

sick with a bug and all that sort of thing (Mentor on school-based PGCE course).

Once you get into school it is the real world isn't it? It's alright hypothesising in lectures but when you get into schools it is a totally different ballgame. Somebody doesn't turn in on the day, you are thrown in at the deep end and anything can happen. These are the sorts of things you don't think about, you are not taught at college how to cope with an emergency (Headteacher on school-based PGCE course).

Thus there seemed to be a noticeable distinction between mentors' perceptions of the 'real' job of the teacher, and perceptions held by the universities. To mentors it meant dealing with teaching in unpredictable contexts characterised by unplanned situations and frequent frustrations rather than understanding how children learn, whereas the university's perception of the 'real' job of the teacher was constructed around a much more reflective, critical, theoretical model which valued and promoted the concept of the student as both teacher and learner.

Rationalising partnership schemes

All this leads again to the conclusion that multicultural education will not be a focal point for beginning teachers on school-based courses in predominantly white areas of the country. In the long-term, what is needed is an ongoing learning community between students, teachers, and HEIs in which roles are clearly defined and a more critical level of discourse which is applied as part of the core curriculum for ITE. The schools' perception of the ITE relationship needs to be resolved. Currently, schools seem to be responsible for practicalities such as the organisation and selection of resources, while HEIs are expected to cover 'the major current theories on how children learn and about the influence on learning of social class and cultural dimensions' (Downes, 1996 p87). Secondly, measures must be taken to ensure that beginning teachers are placed with practising teachers and mentors who can and do articulate a professional conception of teaching that goes beyond the transference of immediate and measurable skills, and who demonstrate a professional commitment to bring 'theory' to bear in the classroom situation. This is not a simple task, as my own mentor experience earlier revealed, and will certainly not be achieved until the TTA endorses such interaction.

Thirdly, the issue of the student's role in school similarly needs to be clarified. Students (by definition) need to be learners, but the drive of school-based training is to push them into the role of 'teacher' for the bulk of their initial education. Heads who take on long-term student placements to place 'bodies' in front of children so that teachers can deal with management activities are doing a disservice to students, to children and to the teaching profession. Time and guidance should be provided to foster a sense of critical reflection that goes beyond the practical organisation and transmission of subject materials. However, recent studies of relationship analysis between mentors and beginning teachers suggests that a school-based context offers only two available forms of conversational relationship: either teacher-pupil or teacher-teacher:

> In identifying which of these types of interaction is open to them student teachers have very little choice. They are immediately positioned in teacher-teacher conversations as competent practitioners who have to prove that competence whenever possible (Edwards, 1997 p29).

There remains an important role for the university tutor. Although the mentor may be best placed to guide the student towards the initial stages of professional competence in the classroom, the university tutor's role is not limited in this way (Hirst, 1990). Primary teachers and researchers have noted that there is a point where beginning teachers reach a distinct plateau in their practice (Furlong and Maynard, 1995), and this is surely where the university tutor comes in (Maynard, 1996). The university tutor's role would be one of negotiated intervention to develop the more critical discourses that beginning teachers need if they are to achieve a meaningful level of professional understanding. This still means that university tutors should make it their business to understand the nature and value of multicultural education and bring it into the professional discourse. My data does not indicate that such tutors are common in the 'white highlands', so relevant training would have to be mandatory. Some students would not necessarily accept the relevance of these issues for their classrooms, so it should be a curriculum requirement and not an option.

At present, the pressures on university tutors to conform to a content driven curriculum of ITE has meant reduced energies to study the social effects of learning. In many departments, with a few notable exceptions, it has been claimed that the *majority* of tutors 'remain as ignorant as their students on the matter of equality issues' (Siraj-Blatchford, 1994 p145, Eggleston, 1993 p13). Rather, my research suggests that often university tutors are conscious of equality issues but feel frustrated because they can find no ways to incorporate the issues meaningfully into their teaching schedules whilst meeting the needs of training criteria. Being conscious of the issues seems to bring with it a wariness about bringing them into the open and an acknowledgement of the potential for misrepresentation, so that lecturers feel they need to be more knowledgeable before tackling the subject. It is disturbing to see how little some students were affected by what input was discernible in their teacher education. One of my set questions to tutors was 'What do you think these students will learn about race during the course of their initial training?', to which typical answers were:

(Silence)

I don't know.

I don't think they are learning an awful lot in the course that they are doing at the moment. Sadly.

If you haven't been alerted to it, or the school that you go to doesn't see it as an issue, because it isn't an issue particularly within their environment, then you know, if you ever move on, you are not going to be aware of those things. So how can you deal with it?

I don't think we can hope to do very much at all in a year and I think that is partly why it is important that we recruit the right kind of people.

The responses of some of the university tutors to my questions are revealing. One of the two course leaders refused to be taped in interview despite my assurances of anonymity and the offer of full respondent validation. He said: 'Not on your life. I'm not going on tape for anything', although he agreed to let me make notes as we talked. It then took me almost six months to get him to agree to an interview. I was given a date, arrived ten minutes early, and waited

41 minutes for him to appear. As he walked out of an adjoining room he informed me that he was in the middle of a lecture, that his students were currently watching a film, and that I could talk to him while it was showing. During our eleven minute conversation he insisted that multicultural education 'certainly' featured as a part of his course, citing as evidence the video his students were watching, which was about Jamaica. He claimed that the film was dealing with the issue of multiculturalism at several levels because: 'it had black people in it, the people spoke in English and the climate is different'. This, he said, was helping to develop 'an awareness of the world rather than just Britain'.

Sara's supervising tutor had this to say about the subject of race and ethnicity:

Maureen	At the moment, on the PG course, I don't know where it gets done. I know where it gets done on the B.Ed course, but on the post-grad course it's (pause). It sort of permeates throughout. There is no (pause) as far as I am aware there is no actual policy that says we do a chunk here and a chunk here and a chunk here.
Russell	Do you think that multicultural education is an issue for schools in all-white areas of the country?
Maureen	I think it is on the same lines as equal opps. They all tend to get muddled up together don't they? Inasmuch as people say 'Yes, it's there, it is implicit in what we are doing. We don't need a separate policy for it'. To a certain extent I can go along with that (pause). So (pause) yes (pause) having said that, awareness needs to be raised if nothing else, but I think in most schools it *is* there. It is *implicit* within the school.
Russell	Is multicultural education something that you discuss with your students out in schools?
Maureen	No
Russell	Not at all?
Maureen	No, it wasn't (pause). I'm guilty of that. I think also, some of the things that happen in the all-white school, I think more schools are now prepared to accept that they need

a (pause) a multicultural policy even though they are an all-white school, whereas at one time they didn't. I think what sometimes happens is that the white traditions often get lost in the going overboard in looking at other cultures, and that's worrying and I don't know if that is because (pause) in England we don't have a lot of traditions (pause). How many traditions do we have that are *English*? Very few.

Russell   But if we went back into history there are hundreds.

Maureen   Yes, but few that we actually celebrate. We celebrate Guy Fawkes (pause). There are very few.

Russell   It is a strange situation.

Maureen   Yes. And yet we go overboard with things like Divali and Asian dance things and (pause) erm I don't know, art work from *other countries*.

Russell   To make sure it is getting covered?

Maureen   Yes. And I must admit it worries me that the English culture, whatever that is, and I'm not sure, is getting lost.

Maureen begins with a general affirmation that multicultural education is worthwhile, and that it is an implicit and permeating element of ITE courses and of primary classrooms, adding that 'all-white schools' have recently begun to see the need for multicultural policies. Then, she appeals defensively to a mythic sense of English 'culture' and finds it 'worrying' that schools are 'going overboard in looking at other cultures'. She supports her 'going overboard' claim by citing Divali and 'Asian dance things' as evidence of the ways in which English traditions have been suffocated. She reveals her 'outsider' mentality by her references to '*other* cultures' and '*other* countries'. Finally, she returns to her 'worry', and the mythic sense of English culture which is desirable, indefinable and ultimately lost. When I discussed this exchange with the university's equal opportunities lecturer, she said:

It alarms me that somebody like that should be a lecturer and should be in power or whatever. That alarms me. It shows (pause) you know, the usual kind of nonsense based on ignorance (omission). I think among the teaching staff, I would hope, certainly among my secondary colleagues that that person is in a minority.

Not so. Maureen's views tally with some of the statements reported to have been made by senior education personnel from the 'white highlands' involved in the AEMS project, such as the Headteacher who suggested that:

> People who live within the Anglo-Saxon culture are being asked to give up everything. Ethnic minorities are not. All movement is towards them (Robinson and Hustler, 1995 p72).

Comments of this kind typify the 'white backlash' to multicultural and antiracist policies that were outlined a decade ago in the Burnage Report (Macdonald *et al*, 1989) and earlier by the Swann Report (DES, 1985). They surfaced strongly again in the media in the wake of the Macpherson Report and its finding of 'institutional racism' in the police and other public services. Yet racism amongst white children is still being accredited to 'high handed approaches to antiracism and crudely designed multicultural policies in schools' (Gardiner, 1997). If multicultural education and multicultural policies still create such a backlash in society and among staff in schools and universities, much needs to be done to ensure that it is effectively addressed as an issue in ITE. When school mentors and supervising teachers believe that this aspect of ITE is the responsibility of the university tutor, and university tutors are increasingly retreating into a politically sanitised, content driven curriculum, the students will miss out on an essential component of their initial training. Until there is national commitment, the current nature of school-based ITE and the persistent problems associated with the 'white highlands' will conspire to limit the understandings of future teachers. Their resulting lack of knowledge, confidence and commitment in this area means that little will continue be done to address an issue that affects us all.

Chapter 7
A typology of disappearance

The students' 'stories' reveal how equality issues in general and race in particular are perceived by beginning primary teachers in predominantly white areas of the country. The four stories demonstrate attitudes and beliefs in the few cases where race was raised as an issue during their training. For the vast majority of my sample this simply was not the case. They had no contact with ethnic minority teachers, lecturers, parents or children, and the equal opportunities input provided by their universities constituted little more than a superficial afterthought or grounds for entertainment. For most of my sample there were no relevant 'stories' to tell, but this in itself is clearly important. In *not* having stories to tell, these students indicate that social justice was treated as irrelevant to their training. Comments were made however, and beliefs were discussed at length during their interviews with me, and this evidence needs to be related here, to contextualise the preceding stories within the overall data.

Bringing the issue of race into the 157 interviews was often problematic. Students, teachers, mentors and lecturers were all happy to discuss issues related to initial teacher training, but seemed surprised when I raised issues of equality and saw it as largely or entirely inappropriate. Time and time again I was informed that there were no ethnic minority children in the school so there was no point in asking such questions. When I asked all the respondents at the end of the year what they thought my research had been about, even after I had raised multicultural education at every interview with every student and taken it as far as I could, only two said they thought there was a multicultural element to my work. The others thought I had been looking at teacher training, or that I had been interested in people generally or had just wanted to see how they developed as teachers. Only one respondent (a teacher mentor) suggested that white children should be part of a wider form of multicultural education – everyone else regarded the whole business of multicultural education as either irrelevant, outdated or dangerous.

As soon as I raised issues of ethnicity during interview, I would be met with a (typically humorous) dismissal. A second or third question about multicultural education would elicit a response that I was simply wasting my time and that there were other (more important) issues to discuss. A metaphorical line would be drawn under that discussion and it was time to move on. Such responses were very similar in tone and in content to the avoidances reported in the previous chapters. A common sense of purpose seemingly exists: issues of ethnicity must be erased from the educational agenda in the classroom, even if this means that any ethnic minority children in the school are similarly 'erased'. A 'typology of disappearance' can be identified, where the range of strategies for ignoring issues of ethnicity becomes formidable in its consistence and overwhelming in its inventiveness.

The most conspicuous spectre that haunted my data was 'silence'. Beginning teachers and the people who train them managed to avoid acknowledging the ethnic status of certain children they taught, or made ethnic minority children somehow white by proxy. The following quotations are drawn from both original transcription data (some from the four 'stories') and from composite responses and behaviours. Contradictions abound, but the following list characterises the various avoidance and proxifying strategies used to make skin colour, ethnic dress, language and culture disappear.

1. We do not have a problem here because we have no black children here.
    The classic perception of ethnicity as a 'problem', followed by a disavowal of ethnic minority presence, even when black pupils are visible in the school.

2. The child is not black because he or she has professional parents.
    These children do not constitute a 'problem' because their parents have highly paid and socially desirable occupations. Black professional parents were spoken of as 'very special people', and 'not stupid at all', implying that had they not been professional people they would have been less 'special' and more 'stupid'.

3. The child is not black because I refuse to see colour as an issue. All people are exactly the same in my eyes and I treat them as such.

4. The child is not black because I refuse to see colour as an issue. All people are different individuals in my eyes and I treat them as such.

5. I refuse to acknowledge she is black because I treat all children as children.

6. I refuse to acknowledge she is black because I am sensitive to her needs. If I openly acknowledged her ethnic identity it would embarrass her. She wants to be just like all the other (white) children.

7. I know he is being abused by the other children but this is not because he is black. It is because he is a 'right little swine'. The other children laugh at him, call him 'Paki' and make derogatory references to his ethnic identity, but this is not because he is black, it is because he not a sociable or likeable child.

8. He is a really sociable and likeable child; all the children in the class 'love' and 'respect' him. I don't see him as black because he fits in with all the other (white) children so well.

9. He does not speak English very well. This is not because he is a member of an ethnic minority, it is because he has special needs and severe learning disabilities.

10. We do not need to acknowledge that the child is black because we have a policy in the cupboard that deals with it.

11. I do not need to see this child as black because I am already sensitive to the issues. I don't need to be told about his needs because you would just be preaching to the converted.

12. I refuse to see this child as black, because if we start to go along that road we will have to start talking about race issues, then we would be writing policy documents, and then there would be a problem where there was none before.

13. We do not need to address ethnic identity because the County's equal opportunities policy covers all that.

14. I do not want to categorise this child as black because I am a Christian, and my faith teaches me how to treat everyone the same way.

15. We do not really want to see these children as black, but we are responding to OFSTED's recommendations and drafting a multi-cultural policy to keep them quiet.

16. There is violence and racist graffiti outside the school gates, but it is not related to the children in this school. Some of them are members of ethnic minority groups, but they are not involved in these disturbances. We do not want to raise it as an issue in case it makes the situation worse.

17. I am not going to make ethnic identity an issue for my classroom because all those racism and sexism problems were resolved years ago. If there is an issue for me to address it would be disability.

18. I do not have time to start dealing with ethnic identity in my lessons, the National Curriculum gives me enough to think about.

19. Issues of race are not in the National Curriculum therefore I don't have to start thinking about them.

20. Issues of race are in the National Curriculum, they are an integral part of the design, meaning that I don't have to start thinking about them.

21. I do not want to deal with ethnic identity as an issue in my classroom because I simply do not want to teach in a school where there are black children.

22. I come from an ethnically diverse area of the country so I do not need to start categorising children as black.

23. We have excellent relations with the County's welfare service who come into school to deal with the ethnic minority children, so I do not really have to think about it.

24. Recognising ethnic identity in the classroom is pandering to the politically correct and teaching black children should just be a matter of common sense.

25. It is not my place to start dealing with things like ethnic identity in the classroom, that sort of theory should be dealt with at college.

26. There simply is not time to start dealing with things like ethnic identity at college, the student learns more effectively when they meet those issues in context while they are out in schools.

27. I am not going to start jeopardising my career by addressing contentious issues like race when it is not something that the university requires me to think about as part of my training.

28. He is not really black but he does have coloured skin.

29. He is black but he's gorgeous, all bright eyed and bushy tailed.

30. It's not that she's black, it's because she's got an attitude problem. The work she has done is fine, she's quite intelligent, but I'm always having to tell her off, and when I've finished she just skips back to her place.

31. I know he is being picked on because he is black, but he gives as good back, so it doesn't matter.

32. I don't want to acknowledge his ethnic identity because he will only use it as an excuse to get his own way.

33. I don't think we should be focusing on the needs of ethnic minority children; we should be concentrating on promoting the traditions of a strong host-nation culture.

34. I don't need to start thinking about how ethnic minorities have been discriminated against. I'm from Liverpool and people discriminate against me because of my accent and my social background.

35. I do not need to deal with racism in my classroom, even if it is overt and violent, because the model set by my teacher/mentor tells me I should ignore it.

36. If I deal with race as an issue in my classroom it will only cause confrontation and will then be counter-productive to effective teaching.

It is not difficult to see why multicultural education is rejected in primary classrooms in predominantly white areas of the country, but it is difficult to ignore the reality of racism. While these students, teachers and lecturers were able to invent and perform conceptual dances to ignore race issues, white children remain as ignorant as ever about social justice and children such as Assan are left to endure repeated ritual beatings and humiliation. My 'typology of disappearance' suggests that not only has racist behaviour in classrooms been systematically ignored but also that institutional practices have effectively managed to spawn an entire generation of teachers who have no understanding of the situation or needs of ethnic minority children, who have no strategies to deal with racist behaviour in the classroom and playground, and who can only conceptualise the issues by convincing themselves that the child is 'not really black'.

This 'typology of disappearance' is predominantly grounded in ITE experiences at primary school level but it is echoed in other research into HEIs. Neal (1995) argues that 'race' as a silent issue takes three forms. Firstly, HEIs are keen to suggest that their equal opportunities policies provide a 'level playing field', meaning that all responsibilities are shifted onto the shoulders of black people themselves. Secondly, black people themselves are racist and this makes the issue more complicated, (again leaving white people free of responsibility). Thirdly, (white) silence is justified by fear of 'saying the wrong thing' and leaving oneself open to accusations of racism. These findings relate strongly to my own data, showing that predominantly white primary schools have become equally adept at turning 'race' into a silent issue in their classrooms and for their beginning teachers.

My four stories trace the relationships between beginning teachers and their mentors, pupils, supervising teachers and university tutors in the context of the shift towards school-based ITE. They may not be unproblematically representative of all forms of ITE but although there was evidence of some good teaching and learning taking place at all levels, there was powerful evidence of serious problems concerning racism and its acceptance as a part of the teaching and learning process. The implicit and explicit acceptance of racism as some form of social phenomenon which is impossible to challenge is carried to the point where some beginning teachers either remain ignorant of how racism operates or feel impotent to deal with it in their staffrooms and classrooms. Thus does racism become a taught element on courses of initial teacher education.

The relationships between the beginning teachers and their mentors (as discussed in Helen's story) suggest that roles, responsibilities and levels of expertise remain problematic. Some schools' un-readiness in their new roles as 'training' institutions was glaringly evident. Mentors were torn between their dual roles and frequently perceived as a cheap form of supply, as Heads manipulated place-ments so as to facilitate space for directed management tasks. This meant that the 'best' teachers were given duties such as policy writ-ing, and the mentors working with students were most often those who had *not* received the mentor training. As a result, the beginning teachers were left to cope with the 'character building' experience of learning 'at the deep end'.

OFSTED uses the language of the collaborative partnership where 'training is a shared responsibility' (OFSTED, 1995 para 48), and the language of the TTA promotes an inclination towards schools becoming more senior within the partnership (Whiting *et al.*, 1996 pp74-77), but the schools and universities involved in my research found themselves speaking different languages. The comfortable mother/daughter relationship between Helen and her mentor had little if anything to do with partnership and much more with a per-ceived need to ensure that Helen could prepare a suitably dif-ferentiated lesson, and that she successfully completed the course. Just as some students adopted a form of strategic compliance in order to get through their school experience, some mentors appeared to be applying similar strategies to hide behind National Curriculum content(ment). Their language bore no resemblance to OFSTED-speak, TTA-speak or even HEI-speak, unless the topic for discussion was ethnicity, where everyone concerned shared the common tongue of accrued silence.

What criteria will be used, then, for improving the suitability of schools and teachers as components of teacher training? The Chief Inspector, Chris Woodhead wants schools that receive outstanding OFSTED reports to be the ones which should take a greater role in the training of beginning teachers (Montgomery, 1996 p8). Will this really be the criterion for school selection? If so, there are other issues to consider. Firstly, it cannot be presumed that schools which receive outstanding OFSTED reports are necessarily going to welcome the chance to become training institutions. Once a school has received such acclamation, it is surely unlikely to want to disrupt its success by bringing in untried elements in the form of long-term students? If parents judge a school by its demonstrable success in the government's league tables, then why should a school jeopardise its status and success to become a training institution?

Nor can we presume that the number of schools that receive outstanding OFSTED reports will equal the number of schools needed for the training needs of the future. HEIs have already found difficulties in generating suitable placements. This implies that either fewer teachers will be trained because there will be fewer suitable schools for placement, or that some students will have to accept training in schools which do not meet the highest standards of OFSTED – which raises serious questions about equity of beginning teachers' learning experience.

The relationships my research revealed between the beginning teachers and their supervising teachers (in the traditional faculty-based context) suggest that there is much to be learned. The notion of race issues as 'no problem here' was prevalent, even when children in the school were being regularly subjected, like Assan, to racially motivated violence. Strategies of avoidance (listed in the typology of disappearance) were common, and not wanting to 'create a problem' was tightly bound with the fear of adversely affecting the school's position within a competitive market place. 'Colour-blindness' therefore became the substitute for equality of provision. Students felt resentment towards their HEIs because their class teachers exploited them as free labour (as happened to Jessica, who was left completely alone throughout her school experience, and to the unnamed student reported in Laura's story who was given a six week full-teaching load so that 'she knew what it felt like'). Little wonder that students are found to be weak 'reflective practitioners' at the end of their courses when their experience in schools seems more like survival training.

The relationships between these beginning teachers and their university tutors were similarly problematic. Some students certainly found their tutors supportive and even inspirational but others felt that they had been badly let down. The university tutors themselves, however, often felt frustrated by the increasing demands on them (such as the tutor I spoke to who could only maintain his school supervisory role by telephone because he had a full, five day teaching commitment at the university). University curricula are pressed into tightly controlled programmes driven to meet specific National Curriculum and training directives, meaning that tutors have fewer opportunities to explore issues such as multicultural education. The equal opportunities sessions which had been arranged were subject to sub-agendas that subverted the process of acknowledging and challenging prejudice. My presence and the research process itself apparently enhanced the amount of provision made: the school-based university ran a co-ordinated four stage programme of lectures and workshops on multicultural education over the course of the year I witnessed, but the following year this was cut to a single afternoon's lecture. The faculty-based university had a single equal opportunities session at the end of my year there, but even this mysteriously disappeared from the time-table the year after I left. A sustained and well thought out programme should be a fixed provision, even when no-one is watching.

The ways that the beginning teachers were seen to relate to their pupils revealed that issues of race, gender, class and disability desperately needed to be discussed in an open and genuinely educative context. Interaction between teachers and ethnic minority pupils remains problematic in terms of academic expectations (Gillborn and Gipps, 1996 pp54-57), in terms of authority relationships

(Sewell, 1997) and in terms of exclusion, where black children are at least five times more likely than their white peers to face permanent exclusion (CRE, 1998). Kim's conception of the (working class) 'stupids' in her care, Laura's experience of the (disabled) child who was left to 'make his own way in life', Assan's ritualised humiliation and the children labelled by their teacher as 'thickos' and 'as thick as pig shit' exemplify the continuation of personal misconceptions, biases and prejudices – all left completely unchecked by any element of the ITE process. Indeed, there were instances where such prejudices were effectively validated as acceptable within the profession and so transmitted to the new generation of teachers.

In addition to all this, some level of culpability rests upon those involved in the multicultural/antiracist education debate. The intense factional in-fighting could have been more productively spent working towards clarification. Antiracism ought not to be seen as a platform for potential academic or social fame but as part of a wider professional commitment towards achieving social justice. As long as writers and activists haggle over minutiae, the absence of a concerted, agreed and authoritative direction which offers meaningful support for educators in the 'white highlands' means that silence (and racism) will persist.

The overriding question this study raises is: 'What about the children?' The business of schools must be to educate the young. School-based training as it now operates means that whole classes of young children receive long-term contact and teaching from people (particularly on the primary PGCE course) who have little or no understanding of the social, emotional, educational and spiritual needs of children. It is pointless for Headteachers to write, as some do, to assure parents that their child is going to spend most of the year not with a student but in the expert care of an 'associate teacher'. Adjusting terminology will not provide children with the education they deserve.

There are obvious steps towards ensuring that school-based training for beginning teachers improves. Communication between schools and HEIs can be enhanced by carefully paced mentor development and the appointment of suitably qualified and experienced link tutors who understand the pitfalls of the mentoring process and can help each side to understand more clearly the needs and skills of the other. Heads need to understand that by accepting long-term placements they also accept a training responsibility, and that 'throwing them in at the deep end' to act as unpaid supply cover and ease the school's staffing budget is unacceptable. Once a placement has been agreed, a training contract should be drawn up between the student and the school. An independent supervisor (drawn perhaps from a seconded team of school teachers and HEI tutors) should ensure that students are engaged with a range of experiences, teaching styles, age groups and ability groups, and that they do not end the course with the presumption that one class or one teaching style is 'typical' of the profession. Placements need also to be more carefully organised and distributed to ensure that – in crude terms – wealthy students who live in affluent areas away from the university are not automatically placed in nearby wealthy schools merely because these are convenient to the university.

Only a huge effort of will at all levels, from national to professional and institutional to individual, can revive the profile of multicultural education. The final chapter indicates some of the ways that all participants can begin to breathe new life into issues of social justice in education.

Chapter 8
Moving forward

My research reveals the shortfalls in new models of 'partnership' education in terms of learning about racial justice, and also in developing reflective and thoughtful teachers who have acquired the commitment and the professional strategies necessary to address these issues. It also points towards areas where improvements can be made to bring about this condition. Research into schools where there are a range of ethnic groups (e.g. Verma *et al* 1994) affords some hope because these are the schools where people have an interest in challenging racism. In the current educational climate, such commitment is less likely in exclusively or predominantly white schools – and this has to change.

Many of the changes that this book has identified need to made at a political and national level.

The government
It is not enough to look at training curricula and simply bolt on a piecemeal statement about respect for other cultures. The whole culture of teaching and teacher training needs to be carefully re-examined. Strict focus on and adherence to the current criteria for providers of ITE and the move into school-based training holds several dangers, particularly at Key Stages One and Two, where teachers are being taught less and less about children. In the drive to make the process of teaching more efficient what is lost is the very foundation for good teaching: the relationship between teacher

and learner. This relationship is not based on measurable outcomes and it is not established by teachers who have had a technicist form of training on lesson organisation and delivery. It is the result of patience, understanding, and sensitivity towards the individual needs of the learners. Within the construction of these relationships lies the potential for effective multicultural and antiracist work to be carried out in our classrooms.

The TTA action plan set out in *Teaching in Multi-Ethnic Britain* (TTA/CRE 1998) concerns itself only with the recruitment and retention of black and Asian teachers (without acknowledging why they find teaching such a deeply unattractive profession). The equivalent of the National Curriculum for those who train teachers are Circulars 10/97 and 4/98 (DfEE 1997 and 1998), and neither of these mentions the need to address equality or multicultural issues. The thrust of documentation at national level is knowledge and skills based, and requires measurable outcomes of all trainees. The section referring to 'Other Professional Requirements' mentions that students should understand their professional responsibilities in relation to the Race Relations Act, but this is clearly addressing a minimum legal requirement, and does nothing to advocate an understanding about racial injustice in education as an essential component of ITE courses.

There have been recent examples of close links between the DfEE, HMI and HEIs in the field of research on race and education and the identification of successful strategies in multi-ethnic schools (Blair and Bourne, 1998). Such work should also be directed to predominantly white schools and the implications of these findings should be built into mandatory requirements for initial teacher education across the UK. Although OFSTED (1999) looked at schools with low as well as medium and high ethnic minority populations, it has no specific recommendations for the practice of such schools in its *Raising the attainment of minority ethnic pupils* and is unlikely to influence their practice.

The last forty years have shown that superficial tinkering and a reliance on permeation has little effect in exclusively white contexts, and children such as Assan are still likely to suffer, but huge, sweeping change through commitment is not imminent. Isolated individual commitment and a watered down, permeated model of multicultural education is insufficient, but unless the findings of the Macpherson inquiry create a sea change in society – which, a few weeks after its appearance, does not look hopeful – the government will opt for rhetoric rather than action. So much will have to be done at the level of the university, the school and the classroom.

University lecturers
Providers of ITE need to accept responsibility for putting race and racial equality back on the training agenda as overt issues to be addressed by all trainees. Although training criteria are continually being tightened, there is now ample evidence to support the need for a compulsory element within training provision where students confront their own beliefs, prejudices and teaching strategies. This will not be achieved by one lecture at the end of the course, neither is it a topic that should be left to any single member of staff. Too often lecturers are awarded the poisoned chalice of equal opportunities, then find themselves ignored, ridiculed or marginalised as all around them things go on just as before.

At present, providers of ITE are experienced in completing mapping exercises so as to keep a wider control of how training criteria are met. The same skills and strategies could be employed by providers to examine closely how they deal with issues of social justice. The student's range of taught sessions, formally and informally assessed assignments and experiences in schools all provide possible starting points for these issues to be incorporated. By completing mapping exercises across entire programmes, providers of ITE could firstly identify the degree to which the student is likely to be asked to address these issues; secondly, ascertain a tighter understanding of when such interventions would be most appropriate and more fruitful; and thirdly, co-ordinate the range of challenges offered over the entire course to ensure that students have opportunities to reassess their earlier responses, attitudes and beliefs in the light of new experience.

Universities should examine their interviewing and enrolment procedures regularly to ensure that potential recruits from ethnic minorities are given the best possible levels of support and advice to encourage them into the profession. The small number of positive role models from ethnic minority groups desperately needs to be rectified and although teaching remains an understandably low career priority for some, those who do want to accept the challenge of teaching should not have to fight their way past layers of institutionalised racist practices.

All members of the training partnership should be particularly sensitive to isolated students from ethnic minority groups, particularly in large group or lecture situations (see Givens *et al*, 1999; Gurewal, 1999). Since completing this work I have seen several lectures given on race issues to audiences of beginning teachers where only one member was black or Asian. These isolated students are potentially vulnerable in these situations, as inexperienced lecturers can look to them unproblematically to validate race issues, making the assumption that the student is able to speak on behalf of entire black or Asian communities. Alternatively, the rest of the student body can exert unwanted pressure on these students, requesting validation of points made by the lecturer and placing them in increasingly dangerous academic and social positions. Wherever possible, lecturers should make it their business to understand the position of the student before any such interaction, and take whatever steps needed to guarantee that undue pressures are not placed on them to 'perform', and that they are not made uncomfortable or further isolated by the teaching process itself.

During my research I noticed that even where entire intakes of beginning teachers are white, many of them have relationships with members of other ethnic groups. Lecturers need to be aware that this is the case and remain vigilant about presuming that the white audience they address have no contact with or understanding of ethnic minority groups. Earlier, I reported that one student reflected on her visit to a mosque and said:

> To a certain extent there is an English way of doing things and I think it should be protected. A good example of that was all that about women

not being allowed into the Mosque if they are menstruating. It's all bollocks.

It would be understandable that an inexperienced lecturer faced with this kind of statement might want publicly to challenge this student's attitudes to race, but there are other considerations to be taken into account. It was only during the last ten minutes of our last interview when I had known this student for a full year, that she told me about her current long-term relationship with a British-born black man and the arguments this had caused in her family. She had personal experience of exactly what racism meant for her partner, and had completed the entire course without ever discussing his ethnic status or introducing him to any of her peers. The student may well have had lessons to learn, but it would have been inappropriate for the lecturer simply to enter the debate by attacking her as racist.

It has to be accepted as inevitable that permeation does not work as a strategy for teaching race issues at degree or PGCE level. During my data collection I was told:

Multicultural education permeates the whole curriculum area.

There are wonderful opportunities for multicultural education.

It comes right the way through really.

It is an integral part of every course unit.

I have done it in the past.

I constantly refer to it.

Yet I was unable to identify a single instance when multicultural issues actually did permeate through to a learner in any form. Permeation as a strategy for understanding race issues needs to be written out of course aims (if it ever existed). There needs to be planned, frank yet sensitive discussion around the issues of multiculturalism and antiracism which allows students in schools and universities to explore their own attitudes and beliefs and to learn more about Britain's diversity of cultures. As long as providers believe that 'someone is doing it somewhere', it will be done by no-one.

It is up to the universities to ensure that students from privileged backgrounds who have never had to challenge their own preconceptions about issues such as ethnicity and social class should not choose where they go for their school attachments. Providers may think they are doing students a favour by placing them near to their homes, or doing the university a favour by saving money on travel costs, but the responsibility for placement cannot be allowed to fall into the hands of the student (as happened with Kim). Those who can afford to travel daily from prosperous areas are likely to be the students who most need to be placed in a social and cultural setting which challenges their views and values. No student has the right to say (as Kim did): 'I do not want to learn about multicultural issues because I simply do not want to teach black children'. Universities need to confront and challenge such statements, not provide institutional loopholes that effectively support them.

It is time to retrieve and re-establish the value for students of studying their own intellectual, philosophical and professional development. With more classroom-based training and the limitations of the one year PGCE, fewer opportunities remain for students to develop as rounded, reflective practitioners. Reading widely and studiously would help overcome this, but teacher training is becoming a time limited exercise, and some students understandably develop the skills that allow them to complete formal requirements with the minimum of commitment, so they can focus on other aspects of their training. Providing the time for students to think carefully about their own development as educators is particularly important at Key Stages One and Two, where so much needs to be known about the matter of childhood. Ideally, postgraduate courses should be longer for teaching in the early years.

Multicultural and antiracist issues should not be decontextualised essay options which students can choose to ignore. They all live in a multicultural and multiracial country. Achieving qualified teacher status should mean becoming a reflective and sensitive practitioner alert to the experiences and needs of all children. This should be every student's aim, and the goal for all their mentors, tutors and lecturers at all stages of their professional development.

Design and delivery of equal opportunities modules and lectures is crucial. This book shows how sessions can so easily be made counterproductive (the lecturer misjudging Rachel), and how easily they can be undermined by students with anti-social justice agendas (Kim's 'games' with the lecturer). Accordingly, the providers of ITE must ensure that those delivering the training are fully aware of the substantive issues to be covered, and that they know just how student resistance to such material can manifest itself during lecture time. The level of knowledge and information of the presenters must be matched by their sensitivity and skill.

Wherever possible, understanding of social issues such as race, gender and class need to be built into models of provision which resist lecture format and instead offer smaller, intimate group sessions where students are unable to hide behind the anonymity of large numbers and are given genuinely supportive opportunities to discuss issues which require careful and often personal feedback.

Teachers and mentors

Just as permeation is destined to fail on degree and PGCE course, it will fail in school-based models of ITE. Whilst universities should accept responsibility for building specific provision into the framework of the course, schools can do much to raise students' awareness of how schools can tackle race issues (for a model at secondary level, see Heilbronn and Jones, 1997). Students and beginning teachers absorb the 'culture' of the school – as this research has demonstrated. Whole school planning can be an effective forum for discussion between mentors and students, drawing out examples where monocultural presentations of society have been resisted, where a range of fictional texts have been used to raise questions about different beliefs and cultures, where the curriculum has been made more inclusive in all subjects, and where antiracist and anti-bullying policies are implemented. The resulting ethos will demonstrate a clear commitment to multicultural aims through the pattern of the children's experience as they pass through the school.

Schools are in many ways ideally placed to illustrate policy formation: how such documents represent collective commitment through agreed principles and how they are designed to support all children. Students should be encouraged to ask questions about the nature of such policies, particularly in white areas, and sensitive support should be given to help them design short and medium term plans which take into account these guiding principles.

Stocks of resources should be overhauled regularly and distributed evenly throughout the school, ensuring that all age groups have access to a range of suitable materials that present a wider view of the world than that of the immediate locality. These resources should then act as part of a formal, ongoing training discourse between mentors and students.

Where there are only a few ethnic minority children on roll, the mentors will have to accept responsibility to understand more deeply the range of particular and specific needs and issues of these children and to communicate this knowledge to students at an early stage. This indicates primarily that the teacher has taken the time to understand and prioritise the child's needs, and communicates a sense of commitment to the student too – a good basis for future planning, discussions with the child and the handling of any potential race related incidents or issues.

There are particular needs in the white areas of the country which are simply ignored at national policy level. The notion that a 'colour-blind' approach is evidence of equality in the school's provision still persists. Right after this research ended, a Chair of Governors at a local (almost exclusively white) primary school advised me that:

> Anything that comes through the door with 'equal opportunities' or 'race' or 'gender' written on it – put it straight in the bin and get on with the real business of education. It's the only way to get anything done.

Not all members of governing bodies are trained (or even well read) in educational philosophy, so much still needs to be done to enlighten governors about racial equality in education. Newly appointed governors should undergo some period of training, one element of which should be a clear and mandatory session on issues of race and racism. While this provision is currently not mandatory, schools can take the initiative to locate effective training and begin the process of educating their governing bodies.

If teachers are to be made more responsible for the professional development of the students in their classrooms, the partnership process needs to be rigorously monitored. The teachers selected to train students should certainly not be those whom Heads deem to be 'most expendable' – so that their most valued staff can be free for other duties. While I was completing this research I worked for a year on an educational management course, where I discovered that Heads were sending teachers on courses that they knew were beyond their capabilities and allocating students to teachers they knew did not have the skills to make the attachment successful. When Heads place students with teachers – for whatever reason – knowing that the relationship will fail, they jeopardise the future prospects not only of the student but also of the profession. And they show little concern for the pupils in their care.

In a similar vein, it now seems to be common (unspoken) practice for student placements to coincide with sick leave. It is difficult to ignore the number of times that students achieve a level of professional practice in their first two or three weeks in a school only to find that the teacher or mentor responsible for their progress then takes sick leave, safe in the knowledge that they are not incurring cost to a supply budget. Heads have not been unknown to plan their student attachments to coincide with the time that their staff members require hospital treatment and periods of convalescence. They may be responding in a practical way to the contemporary economic nature of education, but they are wilfully disregarding students' professional development.

Students should not be placed under the wing of teachers who demonstrate ignorance or hostility towards other cultures (as was clearly evident from my research). Most teachers are aware of the need to develop teaching qualities other than technical transmission skills in the classroom, but they are afforded little time or support for challenging students' attitudes or demanding attention to theoretical or social issues. The training process needs to value and validate such learning, and at school level teachers can be instrumental in bringing issues such as class and racial prejudice onto the agenda and ensuring that there is a requirement for documentary evidence that such considerations have been taken into account in the student's planning and lesson delivery.

As schools take a more active and vociferous role in the preparation of students, they can help establish a clear requirement of teacher training that students acknowledge ethnic identities in the classroom, have the sensitivity and the skills to ensure that their classrooms are places where issues of race and ethnicity can be raised in a supportive and informative environment, where black and Asian children are guaranteed safety and respect, where white children have the opportunity to learn about cultures different to their own and can challenge their own preconceptions and prejudices in a genuinely educative context.

Partnership models between HEIs and schools are becoming more rigorous, and universities are under pressure to listen and respond to the views of partner schools. Documentation which supports the student's experience in schools is open to much negotiation between partners, and schools can begin to insist that race and equality issues feature formally as integral parts of the school experience profile.

Students

Students presumably are in the weakest position of all. To be consistently critical of university and school practices is unlikely to yield positive responses from those who hold the keys to success, but this need not be such a negative scenario.

I have seen – and now demonstrated in this research – that many students enter and leave the training period with a 'colour-blind' approach unchallenged and still in place. The naïve desire to 'treat all children the same' simply does not work. Once racism enters the arena the 'colour-blind' student has to ignore the reasons why a child has faced abuse, so can do nothing to support the child or secure justice. Students should accept it as their responsibility to explore these issues further and part of their personal reading for their professional development should be directed at issues of race and ethnicity.

Whether universities have multicultural or antiracist provision built into their courses or not, students can raise the issues in numerous ways in a variety of contexts. I have noticed for example that certain popular children's poets fail to distinguish between ugly stereotypes and humorous caricatures. Students should feel that they can ask their lecturers questions such as 'What if I had read that poem to my class and one of them was black?' without being too confrontational. Some lecturers will be anticipating the question and will welcome an opportunity to discuss such issues, others will be shaken into questioning their own reasons for selecting such materials.

If their school has no multicultural policy the student can still ask questions about the ways the school recognises and supports the cultural needs of its ethnic minority children, how it promotes a multicultural vision of Britain for all its children and how it would deal with incidents of racism. Students should let it be known that they look to the school for guidance on these matters.

Optional course requirements which offer an equal opportunities element are avoided by students who think the issues are marginal to the business of teaching or fear that they will be at the marking mercy of a politically correct tyrant. Students who want to explore these issues further should look to lecturers they trust and respect to act as advisors even if they are not responsible for the course's delivery.

Students should at all times be sensitive to the experiences of the children in their care. This is primarily a matter of respect, and the beginning teacher should not make assumptions about children's food, clothing, religious beliefs, language or family. My abiding memory of Chani was that she felt she had to draw a picture of meat as her favourite food even though she was for religious reasons a strict vegetarian. While students cannot be expected to know every detail about every child and all the religious and cultural practices prevailing in Britain, they can foster a classroom culture which promotes freedom of expression and sensitively supported discussion by children of their own experiences.

Racism should be confronted every time it arises, but this should be done with the support of the school and students should be wary of acting alone. They should be familiar with policies and codes of practice for handling such incidents. If there are none, they should ask their mentors about possible courses of action. Those who witness racist attacks and are then encouraged to ignore them (as happened to Laura) should seek advice and support.

Fifteen years ago this accusation was directed at white people:

> Your racism has been your silence...Inaction or silence, to me, means action. To me inaction means collusion (Mukherjee, 1984 p6).

As this book goes to print the Macpherson inquiry (1999) into the murder of Stephen Lawrence has accused the Metropolitan Police of 'pernicious and institutionalised racism' and identified racism in other public services also. For the first time in fifteen years there is significant pressure to amend the National Curriculum 'to emphasise the value of cultural diversity, preventing racism from the pre-school age' (McSmith, 1999). Reports claim that 'Racism is inherent in school system' (Ghouri and Barnard, 1999) and statistics now suggest that black boys are up to 15 times more likely to be expelled than their white peers in some parts of the country (Thornton, 1998). The Chair of the CRE has declared that the TTA has been 'negligent' and 'impotent' in its failure to take account of racism in its teacher training curriculum. The front page of the *Observer* of 14.2.99 reported that a government inspector in the school attended by three of the white youths accused of killing Stephen Lawrence, referred to a black male teacher there as a 'nig-nog'.

Macpherson (1999) offers a workable definition of institutional racism, which might sharpen the minds of the TTA and the DfEE. It is, the report says, 'the collective failure of an organisation to provide an appropriate and professional service to people because of their colour, culture or ethnic origin. It can be seen or detected in processes, attitudes and behaviour which amount to discrimination through unwitting prejudice, ignorance, thoughtlessness and racist stereotyping which disadvantage minority ethnic people'.

Inaction has for too long been the strategy of those with the power for change. Silence has been taken to mean that everything is fine – but other powerful silences are revealed in my research. The beginning teachers lacked the will and the ability to recognise, conceptualise and articulate examples of social injustice occurring in front of their (now professional) eyes. In relying on a sense of 'helplessness' and conforming to the (non)strategy of 'What can you do?' this group of newly qualified teachers entered the profession with no understanding of or strategies for promoting equality and little commitment to issues of social justice on which the futures of some of their pupils depend. They had no critical educational philosophy by which to understand the social realities of the children in their care. They were driven by a model of teaching which relies almost exclusively on measurable and demonstrable knowledge transmission, and they had no means of applying a rigorous model of social justice to their classroom practice.

It is the children whose (absent) voices continue to haunt my study; the 'thickos', the 'stupids', the children who are 'as thick as pig shit'. More specifically, the Asian girl in tears at Helen's school, Assan, the boy who 'gets some terrible stick' in Laura's class, and Kamala, who listened to her regular 'tellings off' and then skipped back to her seat. These children were powerless to help themselves, yet it is their lives that are so deeply affected by the inaction of their teachers.

These children's school experiences are the consequence of silence.

References

Ahlquist, R (1992) *Manifestations of Inequality: overcoming resistance in a multi-cultural foundations course* in Grant, C.A. (Ed) *op.cit.*

AMMA (Assistant Masters And Mistresses Association) (1987) *Multi-Cultural and Anti-Racist Education Today* ATL, London (1993 revision)

Anderson, D (1982) *Detecting Bad Schools: a guide for normal parents* The Social Affairs Unit, London

Anderson, L (1994) School-Centred Initial Teacher Training: A Difference of Emphasis Rather than Degree? *Mentoring and Tutoring for Partnership in Learning* 2.2 pp19-24

Anderson, P (1993) Anti-Racists At Odds *New Statesman And Society* 15.10.93 pp18-9

Arnot, M (Ed) (1985) *Race And Gender: Equal Opportunities in Education* Pergammon Press, Oxford

ARTEN (Eds) (1988) *Anti-racist Teacher Education, Permeation: the road to nowhere* Jordanhill College of Education, Glasgow

Ball, S J (1987) *The Micro-Politics of the School. Towards a theory of school organisation* Methuen, London

Ball, S J (1990) *Politics and Policy Making in Education* Routledge, London

Ball, W and Troyna, B (1989) The Dawn of a New ERA? The Education Reform Act, Race and LEAs *Educational Administration and Management* 17.1 pp23-31

Baty, P (1997) TTA is an 'Insult' to the Profession, Dearing Told *Times Higher Education Supplement* 4.4.97 p3

Beardon, T, Booth, M, Hargreaves, D and Reiss, M (1992) *School-Led Initial Teacher Training: the way forward* Cambridge Education Papers Number 2 Dept of Education, University of Cambridge

Blair, M and Bourne, J (1998) *Making the Difference: Teaching and Learning Strategies in Successful Multi-ethnic Schools (Research Report RR59)* DfEE HMSO, London

Blake, D (1993) Teacher Education Reforms? *Forum* 36.2 pp54-56

Blake, D (1994) Progress in the Reform of Initial Teacher Education in England and Wales *Journal of Further and Higher Education* 17.3 pp12-24

Booth, M B, Furlong, V J and Wilkin, M (Eds) (1990) *Partnership and Initial Teacher Training* Cassell, London

Brown, C, Barnfield, J and Stone, M (1990) *Spanner In The Works: Education for Racial Equality and Social Justice in White Schools* Trentham Books, Stoke on Trent

Brown, M (1998) The Unheard Cries *Connections* CRE Summer 1998

Busher, H and Simmons, C (1993) *The Move to School-Based Initial Teacher Education: An Evaluation* Ludoe Publications, Loughborough University, Loughborough

Carter, B and Williams, J (1987) Attacking Racism in Education in Troyna, B (Ed) *op.cit.*

CATE (1989) *Initial Teacher Training: approval of courses Circular 24/89* DES, London

CATE (1993a) *The Initial Training of Primary School Teachers: Circular 14/93 (England) A Note of Guidance* DES, London

CATE (1993b) *The Initial Training of Primary School Teachers: new criteria for courses Circular 14/93 (England)* DES, London

Clay, J and George, R (1993) *Moving Beyond Permeation: courses in teacher education* in Siraj-Blatchford (Ed) (1993)

Coffey, A (1992) Initial Teacher Education: the rhetoric of equal opportunities *Journal of Education Policy* 7.1 pp109-113

Commission for Racial Equality (1992) *CRE Submission to the National Commission on Education* CRE, London

Commission for Racial Equality (1997) *We Regret To Inform You...* CRE, London

Commission for Racial Equality (1998) *Education and Training in Britain* CRE, London

Craft, M (Ed) (1996) *Teacher Education in Plural Societies: an international review* Falmer Press, London

Cross, B E (1993) How do we prepare teachers to improve race relations? *Educational Leadership* 50.8 pp64-5

Crozier, G and Menter, I (1993) The Heart Of The Matter? Student teachers' experiences in school in Siraj-Blatchford, I (Ed) *op.cit.*

Dart, L and Drake, P (1993) School-Based Teacher Training: A Conservative Practice? *Journal of Education for Teaching* 19.2 pp175-189

Delamont, S (1992) *Fieldwork in Educational Settings: methods, pitfalls and perspectives* Falmer Press, London

DES (1984) *Initial Teacher Training: Approval of Courses Circular 3/84* HMSO, London

DES (1985) *Education For All (The Swann Report)* HMSO, London

DES (1991) *School-based Initial Teacher Training in England and Wales: a report by HM Inspectorate* HMSO, London

DES (1992a) *The Reform of Initial Teacher Training* HMSO London

DES (1992b) *Speech of the Secretary of State for Education and Science, Kenneth Clarke, to the North of England Education Conference, Southport 4.1.92* DES Press Office, HMSO London

DfEE (1993) *The Initial Training of Primary School Teachers: new criteria for courses (Circular 14/93)* DES, London

DfEE (1995) *Key Stages 1 and 2 in the National Curriculum* HMSO, London

DfEE (1997) *Teaching: High Status, High Standards (Circular 10/97)* HMSO, London

DfEE (1998) *Teaching: High Status, High Standards (Circular 4/98)* HMSO, London

Donald, P, Gosling, S, Hamilton, J, Hawkes, N, McKenzie, D and Stronach, I (1995) 'No Problem Here': Action Research Against Racism in a Mainly White Area *British Educational Research Journal* 21.3 pp263-275

Downes, P (1996) The Complexities of Initial Teacher Education: the role of higher education in initial teacher training in Furlong and Smith (Eds) *op.cit.*

Eccleshare, J (1991) Trends in Children's fiction in the United Kingdom During the 1980s *Children's Literature in Education* 22.1 pp19-24

Edwards, A and Collison, J (1995) What do Teacher Mentors Tell Student Teachers About Pupil Learning in Infant Schools? *Teachers and Teaching: Theory and Practice* 1.2 pp265-280

Edwards, A (1996a) *Partnerships in School-based Teacher Training: a new vision?* in McBride (Ed) (1996)

Edwards, A (1996b) Possible Futures for Initial Teacher Education in the Primary Phase. Draft paper delivered to 'Exploring Futures in Initial Teacher Education' Conference, Institute of Education, University of London 20/21.9.96

Edwards, A (1997) Guests Bearing Gifts: the Position of Student Teachers in Primary School Classrooms *British Educational Research Journal* 23.1 pp27-37

Eggleston, J (1993) Educating Teachers to Combat Inequality in Verma, G K (Ed) *op.cit.*

Eggleston, J (1995) *Arts Education for a Multicultural Society: an evaluation of the AEMS project* Trentham, Stoke on Trent

Epstein, D (1993) *Changing Classroom Cultures: anti-racism, politics and schools* Trentham Books, Stoke on Trent

Fine, G A and Deegan, J G (1996) Three Principles of Serendip: Insight, Chance, and Discovery in *Qualitative Research Qualitative Studies in Education* 9.4 pp434 – 447

Finn, G P T (1987) Multicultural Anti-Racism and Scottish Education *Scottish Educational Review* 19.1 pp39-49

Furlong, J (1990) School-Based Training: the students' views in Booth, *et al.* (Eds) *op.cit.*

Furlong, J and Maynard, T (1995) *Mentoring Student Teachers* Routledge, London

Furlong, J and Smith, R (Eds) (1996) *The Role of Higher Education in Initial Teacher Training* Kogan Page, London

Gaine, C (1988) *No Problem Here* (revised edition) Hutchinson, London

Gaine, C (1995) *Still No Problem Here* Trentham Books, Stoke on Trent

Gardiner, J (1996a) Teacher Training in School No Panacea *Times Educational Supplement* 19.7.96 p5

Gardiner, J (1996b) Staff May Bear Training Burden *Times Educational Supplement* 9.8.96 p2

Gardiner, J (1997) Pro-Ethnic Policies May Fuel Racism *Times Educational Supplement* 24.1.97 p14

Garner, P (1996) A Special Education? The Experiences of Newly Qualified Teachers During Initial Training *British Educational Research Journal* 22.2 pp155-164

Gentleman, A (1998) No Justice, No Apology *The Guardian* 17.9.98 p1

Ghouri, N (1998) Colour-blind Teaching Condemned *Times Educational Supplement* 17.7.98 p1

Ghouri, N and Barnard, N (1999) Racism 'Inherent in School System' *Times Educational Supplement* 19.2.99 p3

Gillborn, D (1996) Student Roles and Perspectives in Antiracist Education: A Crisis of White Ethnicity? *British Educational Research Journal* 22.2 pp165-179

Gillborn, D and Gipps, C (1996) *Recent Research on the Achievements of Ethnic Minority Pupils* OFSTED, HMSO, London

Gilroy, D P (1992) The Political Rape of Initial Teacher Education in England and Wales: A JET Rebuttal *Journal of Education for Teaching* 18.1 pp5-22

Givens, N, Almeida, D, Holden, C and Taylor, B (1999) Swimming with the Tide; ethnic minority experiences in initial teacher education *MCT Multicultual Teaching* 17.2 pp.30-36

Glover, D, Gough, G, Johnson, M, Mardle, G and Taylor, M (1994) Towards a Taxonomy of Mentoring *Mentoring and Tutoring for Partnerships in Learning* 2.2 pp25-30

Gollnick, D M (1992) *Multicultural Education: policies and practices in teacher education* in Grant, C.A. (Ed) (1992)

Goodwin, J and Wellings, A (1992) Children as Critics: Evaluating Bias in Books in Routh, C (Ed) *op.cit.*

Gordon, P and Klug, F (1986) *New Right, New Racism* Searchlight, Nottingham

Grant, C A (Ed) (1992) *Teacher Education in Research and Multicultural Education* Falmer Press, London and New York

Griffiths, M and Troyna, B (1995) *Antiracism, Culture and Social Justice in Education* Trentham Books, Stoke on Trent

Grinter, R (1994) The Multicultural Dimension in the Primary National Curriculum in Verma, GR and Pumfrey, PD (Eds) *op.cit.*

Grinter, R (1995) *Educating for Equality Through the National Curriculum: A Guide to Opportunities in Subject Teaching* Didsbury School of Education, Manchester Metropolitan University

Grinter, R (1997) Using the National Curriculum to Educate for Equality in Shah, S (Ed) *op.cit.*

Grundy, S and Hatton, E J (1995) Teacher Educators' Ideological Discourses *Journal of Education for Teaching* 21.1 pp7-24

Gurewal, G (1999) Experiences of Racism in Initial Teacher Education *MCT Multicultural Teaching* 17.2 pp17-23

Hargreaves, L, Comber, C and Galton, M (1996) The National Curriculum: can small schools deliver? confidence and competence levels of teachers in small rural primary schools *British Educational Research Journal* 22.1 pp89-99

Hatcher, R (1987) Race and Education: two perspectives for change in Troyna, B (Ed) *op.cit.*

Haydn, T (1997) Problems and Equal Opportunities in Initial Teacher Education in Shah, S *op.cit.*

Hazareesingh, S (1992) The Building Blocks of History in Routh, C (Ed) *op.cit.*

Heilbronn, R and Jones, C (1997) New Teachers in an Urban Comprehensive; learning in partnership. Trentham, Stoke on Trent

Hill, D (1994a) Teacher Education and Training: A Left Critique *Forum* 36.3 pp74-76

Hill, D (1994b) Initial Teacher Education and Ethnic Diversity: cultural diversity and the curriculum in Verma, GK and Pumfrey, PD (Eds) *op.cit.*

Hill, D (1997) Critical research and the Dismissal of Dissent: a brief autobiography *Research Intelligence* Feb 1997 pp25-6

Hirst, P H (1990) The Theory – Practice Relationship in Teacher Training in Booth *et al.* (Eds) *op.cit.*

Hix, P (1992) *Kaleidoscope: themes and activities for developing the multicultural dimension in the primary school* Hampshire Education Authority

Hlebowitsh, P and Tellez, K (1993) Pre-Service Teachers and their Students: early views of race, gender and class *Journal of Education for Teaching* 19.1 pp41-52

Hodgkinson, K (1992) *A Study Of Student Roles and Personal Relationships During Primary School Teaching Practice* Loughborough University Department of Education, Loughborough

Hughill, B (1987) Dramatic Steps That Will Carry Britain Forward *Times Educational Supplement* 16.10.87 p12

Jeffcoate, R (1985) Anti-racism as an Educational Ideology in Arnot, M (Ed) *op.cit.*

Johnson, A and Myers, P (1994) Anti-Racist Body Riven by Personality Clashes and Factional Fighting *The Guardian* 5.11.94 p4

Jones, K (1989) *Right Turn: The Conservative Revolution in Education* Hutchinson Radius, London

Jones, R J (1991) Multicultural Education and the All-White Primary: the effects of a multicultural initiative on perceptions, practices and policies in a rural, all-white primary school. Unpublished M.Ed Thesis, Crewe and Alsager College of HE, November 1991

Jones, R (1997) White Beginning Teachers' Experiences of Race during their Training in the 'White Highlands'. Paper presented to the joint CRE/TTA Conference 'Teaching in Multiethnic Britain', Wolverhampton University, Dec 1997

Jones, R (1998a) Multicultural Education is Dead. Paper presented to British Education Research Association, Queens University, Belfast August 1998

Jones, R (1998b) Deafening Silence: telling stories of beginning teachers' understandings of ethnicity. Unpublished PhD thesis Manchester Metropolitan University January 1998

Kerry, T and Farrow, J (1996) Changes in Initial Teacher Training Students' Perceptions of the effectiveness of School-Based Mentoring over time *Educational Studies* 22.1 pp99-110

King, A S and Reiss, M J (Eds) (1993) *The Multicultural Dimension of the National Curriculum* Falmer Press, London

Klein, R (1995a) Where Prejudice Still Flares Into Violence *Times Educational Supplement* 6.1.95 p9

Leicester, M (1989) *Multicultural Education from Theory to Practice* NFER-Nelson, Windsor

Lewis, S (1997) Black Beginning Teachers' Experiences of Race as an Issue. Paper given to 'Reforming Teacher Education: Innovations in Curriculum and Partnership' conference, NEWI

Liston, D P and Zeichner, K M (1987) Reflective Teacher Education and Moral Deliberation *Journal of Teacher Education* Nov-Dec 1987 pp2-8

Lowe, R (1995) Time to Rebuild? Ways of reconstructing Initial Teacher Education *Forum* 37.3 pp91-2

Lunt, N, McKenzie, P, and Powell, L (1993) 'The Right Track'. Teacher Training and the New Right: change and review *Educational Studies* 19.2 pp143-161

Lynch, J (1987) *Prejudice Reduction and the Schools* Cassell Educational, London

McBride, R (Ed) (1996) *Teacher Education Policy: some issues arising from research and practice* Falmer Press, London

McCulloch, M and Fidler, B (Eds) (1994) *Improving Initial Teacher Training?* Longman, Harlow

Macdonald, I, Bhavnani, R, Khan, L and John, G (1989) *Murder in the Play-ground: The Burnage Report* Longsight Press, London

Macpherson, W (1999) *The Stephen Lawrence Inquiry* Stationery Office, London

McSmith, A (1999) Lawrence: Met Boss Under Threat: Leaked Home Office report accuses London police of 'pernicious and institutionalised racism *The Observer* 21.2.99 p1

Malik, R (1995) Not Ready to Wave a White Flag *Times Educational Supplement* 28.7.95 p7

Mann, N (1994a) Black and White Disunite and Fight *New Statesman And Society* 2.9.94 pp16-7

Mann, N (1994b) Fighting Talk *New Statesman And Society* 18.2.94 p21

Manning, J (1997) Equality Issues and the Teaching of Geography and History in the Primary Classroom in Shah, S (Ed) *op.cit.*

Matthews, J (1992) It's Alright Miss Init?: racial abuse in secondary schools *Multicultural Teaching* 10.2 pp27-35

Maynard, T (1996) The Limits of Mentoring: the contribution of the higher education tutor to primary student teachers' school-based learning in Furlong and Smith (Eds) (1996)

Menter, I (1992) The New Right, Racism and Teacher Education *Multicultural Teaching* 10.2 pp6-9

Menter, I and Whitehead, J (1995) How Partnership Works in Practice *Times Educational Supplement* 7.7.95 p12

Modgil, S, Verma, G K, Mallick, K and Modgil, C (Eds) (1986) *Multicultural Education: The Interminable Debate* Falmer Press, London

Montgomery, J (1996) 'Dump Bad Teachers' *Times Educational Supplement* 21.6.96 p8

Mukherjee, T (1984) I'm Not Blaming You *Multicultural Teaching* 2.3 pp5-8

Neal, S (1995) A Question of Silence? Antiracist discourses and initiatives in Higher Education: two case studies in Griffiths, M and Troyna, B (Eds) *op.cit.*

National Union Of Teachers and the University Of The West Of England, Bristol (1995) *Learning the Lessons: reform in initial teacher training* (no location given) July 1995

National Union Of Teachers (1996) *Anti-Racist Curriculum Guidelines* NUT, London

Newbold, D (1997) Teacher Education – innovation in curriculum and partnership – thoughts on current trends. Paper given at NEWI conference, Wrexham: 'Reforming Teacher Education: Innovations in Curriculum and Partnership' 24-27th March 1997

OFSTED (Office for Standards in Education) (1993) *The Training of Primary School Teachers* HMSO, London

OFSTED (1995) *Partnership: Schools and Higher Education in partnership in secondary Initial Teacher Training* HMSO, London

OFSTED (1999) *Raising the attainment of minority ethnic pupils – school and LEA responses* OFSTED, London

O'Hear, A (1988) *Who Teaches the Teachers?* The Social Affairs Unit, London

O'Keeffe, D (1990) *The Wayward Elite* Adam Smith Institute, London

Ousley, H (1998) Black Exclusion Scandal *Times Educational Supplement* 18.12.98 p13

Pallister, D (1998a) Met Denies Racism Over Lawrence *The Guardian* 18.9.98 p4

Pallister, D (1998b) Black Victim's Family Fights for Facts *The Guardian* 18.9.98 p4

Parekh, B (1986) The Concept of Multicultural Education in Modgil, S *et al* (Eds) *op.cit.*

Patel, K (1994) *Multicultural Education in All-White Areas* Avebury, Aldershot

Pearse, S (1989) Addressing Race and Gender in Rural Primary Schools Using

Two Case Studies *Gender and Education* 1.3 pp273-281

Phillips, T (1998) Why is the Face of Exclusion so Black? *Times Educational Supplement* 23.10.98 p15

Pyke, N (1995a) Inspections 'Neglect' Racial Equality *Times Educational Supplement* 3.2.95 p3

Pyke, N (1995b) School-based Training Under Pressure *Times Educational Supplement* 28.7.95 p3

Pyke, N (1996) Ministers Attacked Over Race Research *Times Educational Supplement* 3.5.96 p1

Radnor, S J (1997) Equal Opportunities Education in the Primary Initial Teacher Education Partnership in Shah, S (Ed) *op.cit.*

Rafferty, F (1996) Ethnic Gap Growing in Many Areas *Times Educational Supplement* 6.9.96 p3

Rafferty, F and Dean, C (1996) Heads Back Training Reform *Times Educational Supplement* 13.12.96 p1

Ribbins, P and Sherratt, B (1997) *Radical Educational Policies and Conservative Secretaries of State* Cassell, London

Richardson, R (1999) Unequivocal Acceptance – lessons from the Stephen Lawrence Inquiry for education. *Multicultural Teaching* 17.2 pp7-11

Robinson, J and Heyes, I (1996) Conflicting Models of Teacher Training in Multi-Ethnic Classrooms: journal of a mentor *Language, Culture and Curriculum* 9.2 pp120-132

Robinson, J and Hustler, D (1995) Celebrating Naivety: the role of black artists in multicultural and anti-racist education *Curriculum Studies* 3.1 pp61-77

Routh, C (Ed) (1992) *Cultural Mosaic: the multicultural dimension in the National Curriculum* University of Reading

Sewell, T (1997) *Black Masculinities and Schooling: How Black boys survive modern schooling* Trentham, Stoke on Trent

Shah, S (Ed) (1997) *National Initiatives and Equality Issues* University of Hertfordshire, Watford

Singh, E and Gill, D (1991) *No Racism Here! (We Treat Them all the Same)* Association for Curriculum Development/ILEA Multiethnic Inspectorate, London

Siraj-Blatchford, I (1991) A Study of Black Students' Perceptions of Racism in Initial Teacher Education *British Educational Research Journal* 17.1 pp35-50

Siraj-Blatchford, I (1993a) Racial Equality and Effective Teacher Education in Siraj-Blatchford, (Ed) *op.cit.*

Siraj-Blatchford, I (1993b) Social Justice and Teacher Education Inequality and Teacher Education in Verma (Ed) *op.cit.*

Siraj-Blatchford, I (1994) *The Early Years: laying the foundations for racial Equality* Trentham, Stoke on Trent

Siraj-Blatchford, I (Ed) (1993) *Race, Gender and the Education of Teachers* Open University Press, Buckingham

Siraj-Blatchford, I and Troyna, B (1993) Equal Opportunities, Research and Educational Reform: some introductory notes *British Educational Research Journal* 19.3 pp223-225

Sparkes, A C and MacKay, R (1996) Teaching Practice and the Micropolitics of Self-Presentation *Pedagogy in Practice* 2.1 pp3-22

Taylor, B (Ed) (1987) *Ethnicity and Prejudice in 'White Highlands' Schools Perspectives*, University of Exeter, Exeter

Taylor, W H (1990) Multicultural Education in the 'White Highlands' After the 1988 Education Reform Act *New Community* 16.3 pp369-378

Teacher Training Agency (TTA) (1997) *Training Curriculum and Standards for New Teachers* (Consultation document Feb 1997) TTA, London

Thornton, K (1998) Blacks 15 Times More Likely to be Excluded *Times Educational Supplement* 11.12.98 p1

Tomlinson, S (1993) The Multicultural Task Group: the group that never was in King, A and Reiss, M (Eds) *op.cit.*

Tomlinson, S (1996) Teacher Education for a Multicultural Britain, in Craft, M (Ed) *op.cit.*

Travis, A (1995) Truth That's Hard To Figure Out *The Guardian* 16.8.95 p22

Troyna, B and Williams, J (1986) *Racism, Education and the State* Croom Helm, Beckenham

Troyna, B (1987) Beyond Multiculturalism: Towards the Enactment of Anti-Racist Education in Policy, Provision and Pedagogy *Oxford Review of Education* 13.3 pp307-320

Troyna, B (Ed) (1987) *Racial Inequality in Education* Tavistock, London

Troyna, B (1993) *Racism And Education* Open University Press, Buckingham

TTA/CRE (1998) *Teaching in Multi-Ethnic Britain: a joint report by the teacher training agency and the commission for racial equality* CRE, London)

Tysome, T (1996a) Teacher Training Set For A Rethink *Times Higher Education Supplement* March 15th 1996 p3

Tysome, T (1996b) Teaching Courses set A Price List *Times Higher Education Supplement* March 22nd 1996 p3

Tysome, T (1996c) Whitehall To Run Teacher Training *Times Higher Education Supplement* June 14th 1996 p3

Verma, G K (Ed) (1993) *Inequality and Teacher Education* Falmer Press, London

Verma, G K and Pumfrey, P D (Eds) (1994) *Cultural Diversity and the Curriculum Volume 4: cross-curricular themes and dimensions in primary schools* Falmer Press, London

Verma, G, Zec, P and Skinner, G (1994) *The Ethnic Crucible: harmony and hostility in multi-ethnic schools* Falmer Press, London

Weston, C (1989a) Minority Groups call for end to Anti-Racist Education *The Guardian* 8.2.89 p5

Weston, C (1989b) NUT Warning on Anti-Racist Zeal *The Guardian* 14.3.98 p8

Whalley, D (1987) Multicultural Education – Making A Start in Taylor, B (Ed) (1987)

Whitehead, J, Foster, T and Blight, M (1994) The PGCE and the Training of Primary Teachers in McCulloch, M and Fidler, B (Eds) *op.cit.*

Whiting, C, Whitty, G, Furlong, J, Miles, S and Barton, L (1996) *Partnership in Initial Teacher Education: a topography* Modes of Teacher Education Project (no location given)

Williams, E A (1994) Roles and Responsibilities in Initial Teacher Training – Student Views *Educational Studies* 20.2 pp167-180

Wilson, J (1991) Does Equality (Of Opportunity) Make Sense In Education? *Journal of Philosophy of Education* 25.1 pp27-31

Wilson, J (1993) Equality Revisited *Journal of Philosophy of Education* 27.1 pp113-114

Younge, G (1995) Black in Britain in *The Guardian* 2 20.3.95 pp1-4

Index